Millard, Anne

How people lived

HOW PEOPLE LIVED

Written by
Dr Anne Millard

Illustrated by
Sergio

DORLING KINDERSLEY, INC.
LONDON · NEW YORK · STUTTGART

DK

A DORLING KINDERSLEY BOOK

Editor Jane Elliot

Series Art Editor Roger Priddy

Series Editor Angela Wilkes

Managing Editor Vicky Davenport

Revised American Edition, 1993
10 9 8 7 6 5 4 3 2 1

Published in the United States by
Dorling Kindersley, Inc., 232 Madison Avenue
New York, New York 10016

 Published in Great Britain by Dorling Kindersley Limited.
Distributed by Houghton Mifflin Company, Boston.

ISBN 1-56458-237-X

Library of Congress Catalog Card
Number 92-54315

Phototypset by SX Composing Ltd, Rayleigh, England
Reproduced in Singapore by Colourscan
Printed in Spain by Artes Graficas, Toledo S.A.
D.L.TO:1785-1992

CONTENTS

PEOPLE FROM THE PAST

Over the years, people's basic needs have changed little. In this book, you can join your ancestors from thousands of years ago as they emerged from their caves wearing animal skins. Or you can go back hundreds of years and see a banker in his house, dressed in rich clothes and furs. Both the caveman and the banker have things in common with each other and with us becuase we all have similar needs, such as food, clothing, and shelter.

Although people have always needed protection from the burning sun or the bitter cold, their shelter and clothing have changed over the years. People soon learned that food tasted better if it was cooked over fire and that they could grow food for their families and animals.

Through the pages of this book you will see how your ancestors lived, discover their likes and fears, and explore their houses, which have been drawn to let you see inside.

Meet the people

Here are some of the people you will meet in this book. Some are extremely tough because of the harsh conditions in which they live, others live in the lap of luxury.

Ban and Uro
You will begin your journey in what is now France, in around 13,000 BC, when Europe is in the grip of an ice age. Find out how Ban and his father Uro survive by hunting for meat with flint-tipped spears.

Illa
Illa lives in what is now Iran at a time when a vitally important change in human history is taking place. It is around 10,000 BC. As she gathers in the harvest, Illa takes part in a new way of life: farming.

Kai and his mother
Kai belongs to a Celtic tribe living in central Europe in about 500 BC. His family are metalsmiths, and he is learning from them. His mother spends hours cooking in their large hut.

Rudek
Rudek is a chief living in about 500 BC in Siberia, near the Altai Mountains. He joins his men herding their horses to new pastures. Life in the saddle is especially hard during the freezing winters.

Lysander and Thea
Around 424 BC, the Greek city of Athens is producing some of the greatest thinkers, writers, and artists known. Thea and Lysander live with their parents and are considerate to their slaves.

Lady Ch'eng
In around 130 BC, the Han emperor's wife lives quietly in a palace with beautiful gardens. But Lady Ch'eng is old and unwell. Sadly, she dies when she goes to inspect her son's new horse.

Rasfa
The new prosperity brought about by farming means that towns grow and people have new needs. In about 6000 BC, the people of Catal Hüyük, in Turkey, start trading. Rasfa is always the first to trade

Ashnan
In Mesopotamia, in about 2050 BC, it is pleasant to live in an organized city where rulers and priests protect and care for you. But there is always a price to pay, and Ashnan's family has to sell her.

Hori
Hori lives in Egypt in about 1480 BC, when the Egyptian civilization is at the height of its greatness. Watch Hori's family take part in a ceremony, and learn how a brother becomes a mummy.

Princess Dictynna
Meet Dictynna, a princess on the Mediterranean island of Crete in about 1480 BC. She lives a life of great comfort in a brightly painted palace. Like the rest of the Cretans, she loves the sea.

Claudius and Livia
Senator Claudius and his family live in a lavish house in the imperial city of Rome in about 20 BC. Although every freeman is a citizen like Claudius, you will see that not everyone lives in such luxury.

Eric
You can find the Viking blacksmith Eric working in a village in Norway in about AD 950. He is a skilled craftsman, and his fine swords are valued by his warrior friends, who plunder distant shores.

Brother William
For Brother William, life in a monastery in AD 1320 combines service to God and to those in need. The medieval monks offer shelter, food, clothing, and medical cave to travelers, the sick, and the poor.

Francesco
In the Renaissance town of San Vitale in AD 1450, you will discover how Francesco spends the money he has made in his bank. He is usually patronizing a new poet or artist, or entertaining.

IN THE SHELTER OF THE CAVE

You have traveled back in time to the year 13,000 BC and find yourself in the Stone Age. You are in a wooded river valley in what is now southwestern France. The climate is much colder than nowadays because Europe is in the final stages of an ice age, and France is rather like northern Russia or Canada are today. It is late summer, and a group of people are setting up camp in the mouth of a cave.

We are directly descended from people like those shown here. The scientific name for them is *homo sapiens*, which means "thinking man," but they are often called Cro-Magnon man, after the cave in France where their remains were first discovered. Like people who lived before them, the Cro-Magnons lived by hunting, fishing, and gathering wild plants to eat. They spent their lives moving from place to place in search of food, living in tents or sheltering in caves. The Cro-Magnons were not just hunters; besides their great knowledge of animals and plants, they left behind many tools, weapons, and paintings, which show that they were skilled artisans and talented artists.

Setting up camp
Here and on the next two pages, you can see the tribe setting up camp outside one of the many limestone caves in the area. Ban belongs to this tribe, and he and his father Uro have been hunting.

Instant housing
Ban's tribe lives in tents in the open for part of the year, but when the winter snows come, the tribe moves the tents into caves, perhaps building a windbreak of stones across the entrance.

Telling tales
Life is hard, and many people die young. Old people are valued members of the tribe who pass on their skills and wisdom to the children. This old man is describing a great hunt.

A blazing fire
A fire has been started using sparks created by striking two very hard rocks, pyrite and flint, against each other. This is quicker than rubbing two wooden sticks together, as earlier people did.

Tent building
Nomads are people who move around the land, setting up camp where they are likely to find food by hunting and fishing. Ban's tribe is nomadic. After arriving at their new location, they pitch tents made from animal hides thrown over frameworks of wooden poles and weighted down with heavy stones.

Thick-skinned
The Cro-Magnons wear warm clothes made of animal hide and fur. They have invented a needle made of bone, so they can sew the animal skins together. They often decorate their clothes with beads, teeth, and shells.

On a knife's edge
The tribe are skilled toolmakers. They use flint to make sharp, efficient blades for their knives, spears, axes, scrapers, and chisellike tools called *burins*. They also make tools from antlers, bones, and ivory. Archaeologists today can tell one group of cave-dwelling hunters of the past from another by their tools.

The hunters' return

It is the end of the day, and Uro and Ban return from the hunt with their kill strung up between wooden poles. These Cro-Magnons hunt mainly reindeer, deer, and wild boar. Every part of the catch is put to good use: the meat is cooked, the hides are made into clothes and tents, and the bones, antlers, and tusks into tools and weapons.

Food for the future

While the men go hunting, some of the women gather plants, roots, and berries in leather bags and rush baskets. They will store these for the winter, when food is scarce.

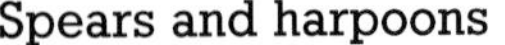

Spears and harpoons

The Cro-Magnons hunt in groups if they are following large animals. They have invented tools to increase their chances of success. These include spear-throwers, which enable them to hurl their spears farther and with greater force, and harpoons that the animals cannot shake free.

How do we know?

We know how important animals were to the Cro-Magnons from the magnificent rock paintings found deep within some of their caves. The pictures, mostly of animals and hunting scenes, may have been done to please the spirits in which the tribes believed and to bring hunters luck.

Fishing with nets
Uro's tribe is equally good at catching freshwater and saltwater fish. They spear the fish with sharply barbed harpoons or catch them in nets held down with small stones.

Beauty from the beasts
Some of these women are making necklaces from shells, animal teeth, ivory, and colored pebbles. Slices of mammoth tusk make good bracelets. The other women are preparing animal skins to make into clothes, footwear, tents, bags, and bedding for the tribe.

Clues to the past
Apart from the cave paintings, the main clues to how the Cro-Magnons lived are provided by the remains of tools and weapons found in their caves. Tools made of flint, bone, antler, and ivory have survived, but anything made from other materials has vanished.

EARLY FARMERS

You have moved on 3000 years in time to about 10,000 BC, when a dramatic change was taking place in the way people lived. For the first time in history, people began growing their own food. This early farming took place in the fertile foothills of the Zagros Mountains, in what is now Iran.

Instead of gathering the seeds of wild grasses simply to eat, people began to save some of the seeds and planted them to produce a crop for the following year. This meant that they settled in one place to tend their crops and then to guard the harvest once it was stored. Over the years, they carefully chose and planted the seeds that would produce the best crops. They began farming legumes (peas and beans) in the same way. They also began to breed sheep and goats to supply meat and milk, so that they did not always have to hunt for wild animals.

People now had a new way of living. Because they were settling in one place, they built permanent houses that were safer and more comfortable than tents. They no longer had to carry belongings around with them so they began to collect possessions.

Thrown to the wind
In the village, they *winnow* the grain by tossing it into the air so that the *chaff* (the outer coating) blows away. They then hide it in pits lined with clay or reeds to discourage theft.

Food from the land
In this scene, you can see these early farmers working on the land. This year's crop is ripe, so Illa and the women harvest it to eat or store.

Daily bread
Their most important food is bread. The women grind the grain between heavy stones to make flour. Then they add water and shape the mixture into round, flat loaves, which they bake in clay ovens.

Harvest home
The women harvest the crop using sickles made of sharp flint blades set in wooden handles. Illa gathers ears of wheat to take to the village.

Breeding animals
Men look after the animals. They have successfuly bred sheep and goats and even tamed wild pigs. Taming the huge, fierce wild cattle to produce milk proves much harder.

Handiwork
The villagers make bowls and tools out of stone and weave baskets from the reeds that grow nearby. They wear clothes made from animal skins roughly sewn together.

Mud houses
This new house is nearly finished. The builders make walls out of mud, gathered in special mud pits, and use ladders to construct the roof from branches covered with reeds, straw, and a layer of mud.

THE FIRST TOWN

From an early village in the Middle East, you have now moved on 4000 years in time to arrive in Turkey in about 6000 BC. This busy and prosperous town is of great importance because it grew from a small village into the first known town.

The town of Catal Hüyük was successful due to trade because its people produced items that were valued highly elsewhere. About 2000 years earlier, pottery and weaving had been invented and the skilled people made clay pots and wove cloth from wool gathered from their sheep. They were also lucky because nearby volcanoes had produced a kind of glass called *obsidian*, and from this they carved extremely sharp tools and even made mirrors. The people also gathered food from the wild and hunted animals for meat and skins.

A town without streets
As you can see, the houses touch each other and there are no streets. There are also no doors; to get inside, people climb a ladder and drop in through a hole in the roof. Nearby, Rasfa is busy trading with the villagers.

Give and take
Money has not been invented yet, so people barter. This means that a person who wants a bowl has to offer something in exchange, perhaps a tool, that the bowl's owner agrees is of the same value. The trading can be very noisy, but good deals are made.

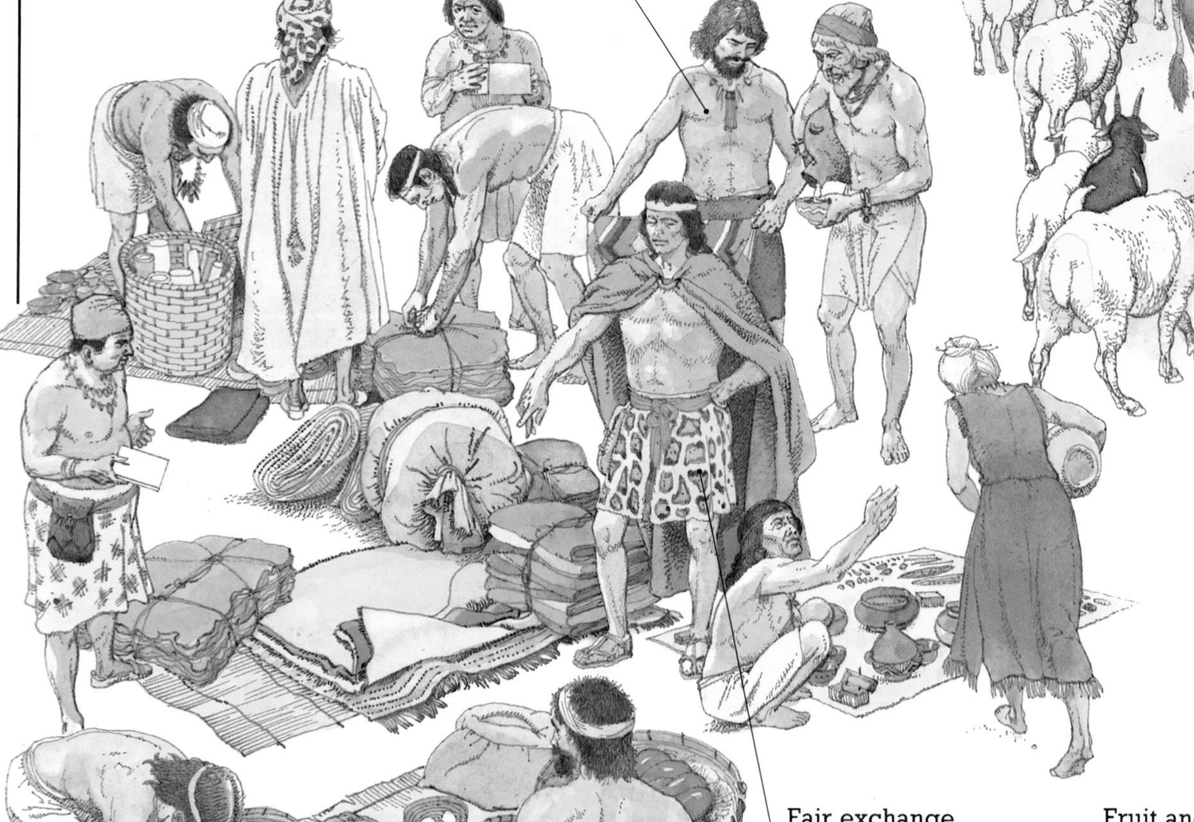

Fair exchange
Rasfa comes from neighboring Syria. He wants obsidian tools and woolen cloth and has shells and good flint to trade. The townspeople need new flints, for starting fires, but they drive a hard bargain.

Fruit and nuts
The farmers grow barley, wheat, and peas. They also gather almonds, acorns, and pistachio nuts, and pick fruit, some of which they make into wine. They breed cattle and sheep, and hunt wild boar and deer for meat and skins.

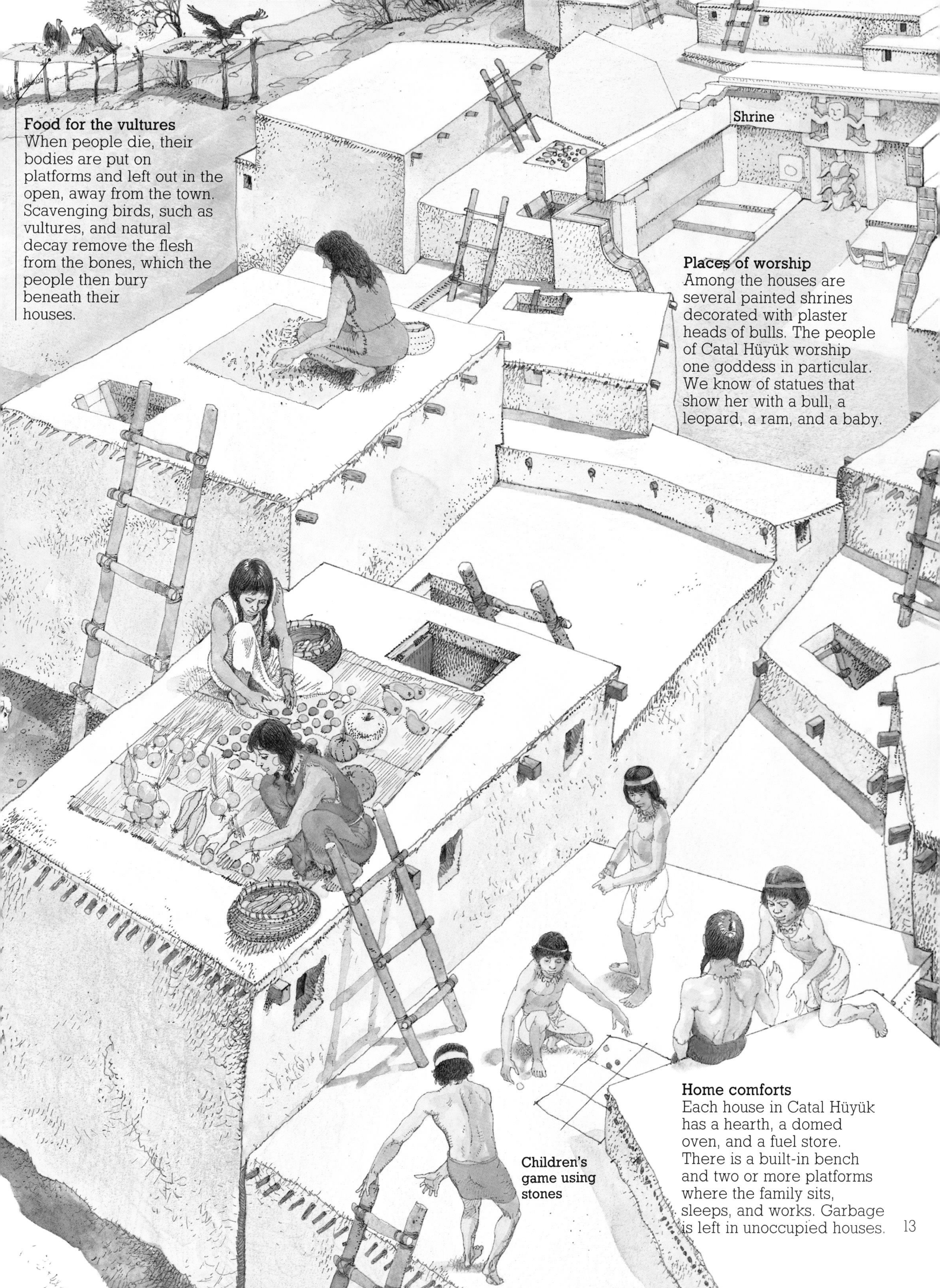

Food for the vultures
When people die, their bodies are put on platforms and left out in the open, away from the town. Scavenging birds, such as vultures, and natural decay remove the flesh from the bones, which the people then bury beneath their houses.

Places of worship
Among the houses are several painted shrines decorated with plaster heads of bulls. The people of Catal Hüyük worship one goddess in particular. We know of statues that show her with a bull, a leopard, a ram, and a baby.

Home comforts
Each house in Catal Hüyük has a hearth, a domed oven, and a fuel store. There is a built-in bench and two or more platforms where the family sits, sleeps, and works. Garbage is left in unoccupied houses.

THE CITY-STATES

From Turkey, you have jumped south again into what is now called Iraq. You are in Sumer (southern Mesopotamia), a large area of very lush country running between the Tigris and Euphrates rivers. It is about 2050 BC, and the temperature is very hot.

Sumer was one of the earliest and greatest civilizations. Archaeological finds show us how inventive the Sumerians were. They created the earliest form of writing and were skilled artists and impressive builders.

Sumer was divided into city-states. The land and people surrounding a city were controlled by the city rulers. People had to pay taxes to the city, and the city organized farms to produce successful crops, either as food or for trade. The wealth of the city-states was largely due to the invention of irrigation, a system for watering the fields, even during a drought.

In the shadow of the city
On these pages, you can explore the outskirts of the great city of Ur, seen in the distance. Although far away, the city controls the lives of the people who work very hard on the land.

The wheel
The Sumerians benefit from a great invention, the wheel. They use wheels to make pots and carts. The noblemen ride in chariots drawn by *onagers* (wild asses), but most people travel by boat or by foot.

Hard times
This family is worried. Last year, they were fined because their sheep strayed and damaged their neighbor's crops. Now they cannot pay the taxes.

Sold into slavery
To save her family, 14-year-old Ashnan is being sold as a slave to the merchant Nesag. He has come from Ur with his servants to buy wool, cloth, grain, oil, and slaves.

Mud and reeds
Reeds and palm trees grow along the riverbanks and are used, along with mud bricks, to build houses. Reeds are used to make fishing boats and cow sheds.

The farmer's lot
Barley is the Sumerians' main food, but they also grow a wide variety of vegetables and fruit. They raise cattle, sheep, goats, pigs, and donkeys. Oxen are used to plow.

How we know
Archaeologists have excavated Sumerian buildings and found decorations inlaid in furniture and pieces of pottery that give us an idea about everyday life.

THE CITY OF UR

You are now seeing the city of Ur. The streets are full of people heading toward the huge temple that dominates the whole city. The mud brick temple is built on top of a *ziggurat*, or tower, dedicated to the moon god Nanna.

The merchant Nesag
As you can see, the merchants prosper in Ur. Stone, metal, and good timber are in great demand. Because these materials cannot be found locally, they are traded from foreign lands. The merchants barter with grain, cloth, and farm produce.

Early bathrooms
As a wealthy man, Nesag has a house with a bathroom and a system of drains. In the kitchen, the slaves work on rush matting, and use metal tools and pottery bowls.

Welcoming a hero
Nesag is giving a party to celebrate the safe return of his son Shulgi, a soldier who has been fighting for the king. Slaves prepare special food, and guests gather to greet their host.

A moon priestess
Geme-enlil is a priestess of the god Nanna. With the help of the new slave, Ashnan, she is dressing to go to the temple, where the king will give thanks for his great victory.

Twisting alleyways
Although Ur has some broad streets, Nesag's house is reached by many narrow alleyways. The mud-brick house is built with two stories and has a central open-air courtyard.

Off to school
Nesag's youngest son is at a school set up for the sons of prosperous parents. The pupils sit on benches in front of the teacher, who is explaining the symbols used in Sumerian writing.

How we know

Clay tablets show us that the Sumarians invented the first writing, now called *cuneiform*. They started by scratching simple drawings into clay; in time, they had a symbol for everything.

ON THE NILE

From a land divided by city-states, you have moved southwest to Egypt. The year is about 1480 BC, and the country is united under one of a succession of powerful kings called *pharaohs*. Egypt is a great civilization, and its people are highly skilled.

Egypt would be a desert if not for the Nile River, which runs through it. Each summer, the Nile River floods, and for several months, water soaks the land. The people developed an irrigation system, as in Ur, which allowed them to farm the fertile land along the river by storing up water from this flooding, or inundation. They grew wheat, barley, and vegetables for food, and flax, which they wove into fine linen cloth. The wealth of Egypt was based on its farming, its gold, and skillfully made goods, which were exported.

A great nobleman's estate

It is early October, and the flood is over. Neb is the steward on one of the large farms owned by Chancellor Nehsi. He has ordered the slaves to work especially hard to control the water.

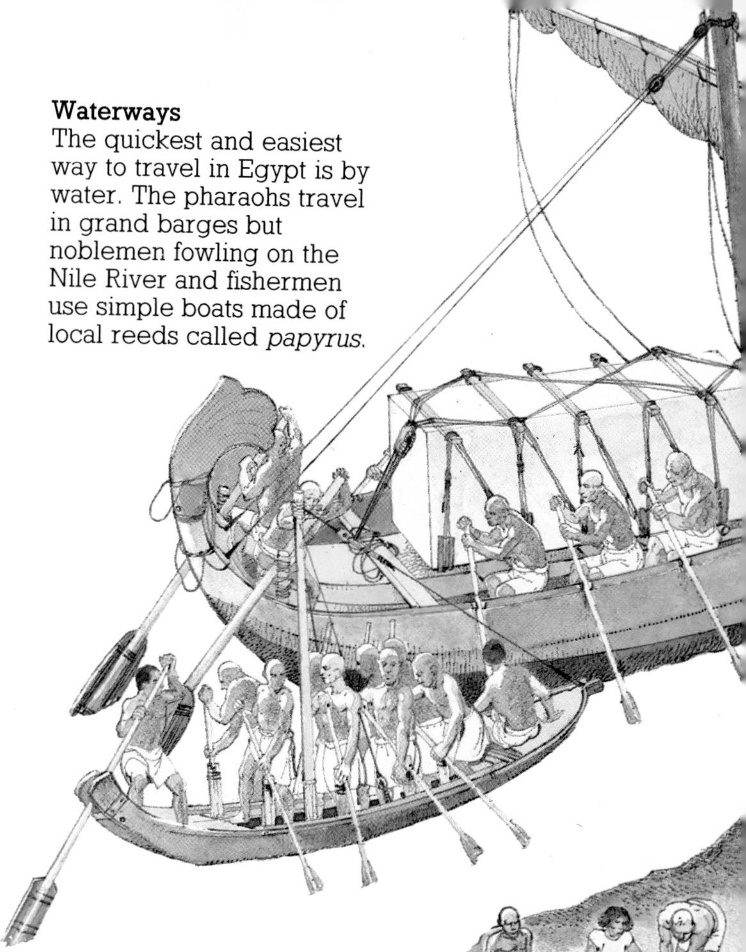

Waterways

The quickest and easiest way to travel in Egypt is by water. The pharaohs travel in grand barges but noblemen fowling on the Nile River and fishermen use simple boats made of local reeds called *papyrus*.

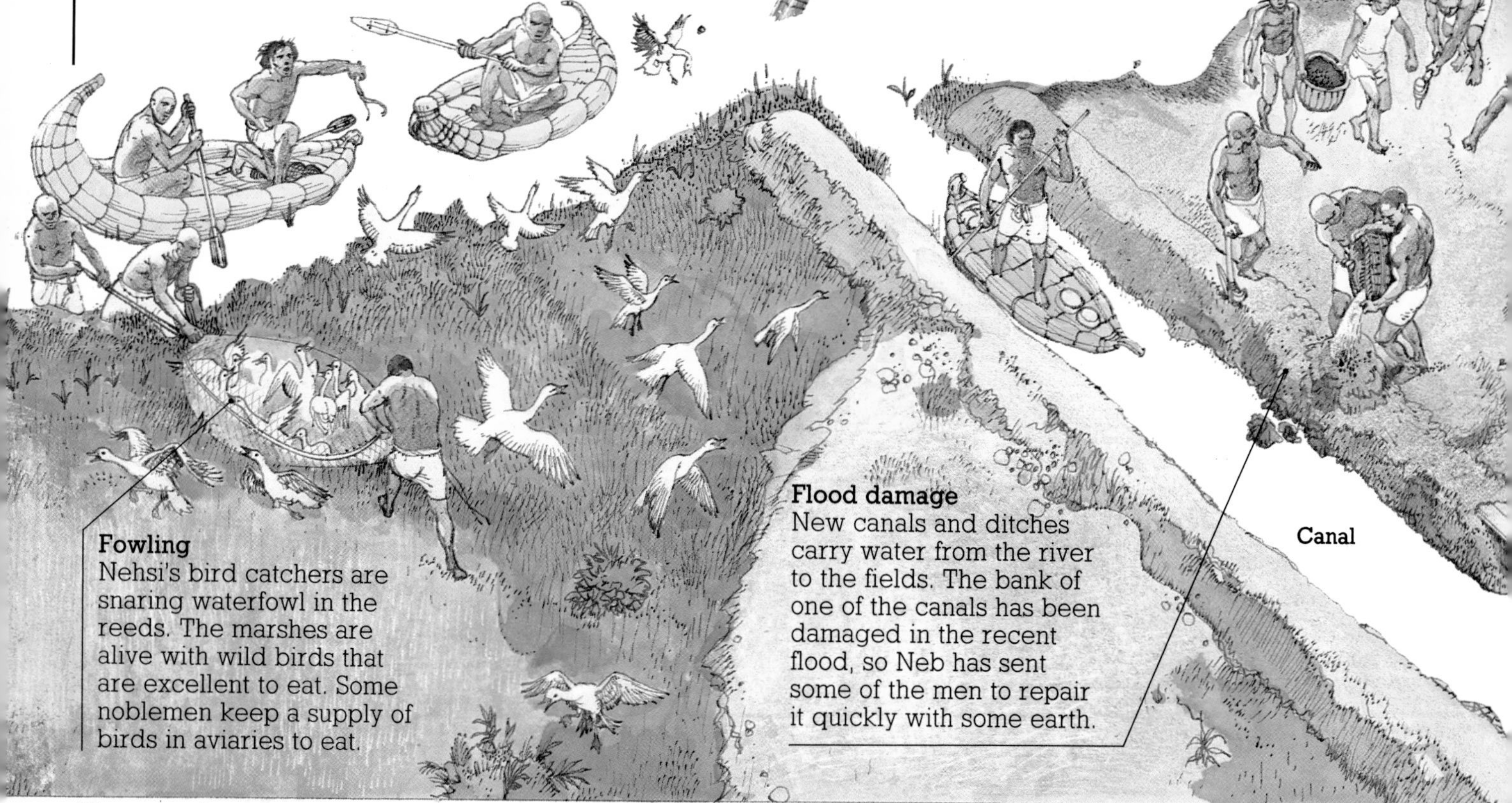

Fowling

Nehsi's bird catchers are snaring waterfowl in the reeds. The marshes are alive with wild birds that are excellent to eat. Some noblemen keep a supply of birds in aviaries to eat.

Flood damage

New canals and ditches carry water from the river to the fields. The bank of one of the canals has been damaged in the recent flood, so Neb has sent some of the men to repair it quickly with some earth.

Canal

How we know

Noblemen in Egypt decorated their tombs with paintings of daily life, so today we know how they lived. This scene shows peasants hard at work as they reap, thresh, and winnow a crop.

Fish food
Another food supply comes from the Nile River, which is rich in fish. The men catch the fish with a hook and line, a harpoon, or, as shown here, nets slung from small boats rowed with oars.

Bursting the banks
The Nile River is Egypt's only source of water. When it floods, the water soaks the fields and deposits a layer of fertile soil called *silt*. Canals hold back the water.

October ploughing
Some men plough the fields, while others follow behind scattering seed in the furrows left by the plow. Animals are driven over the field to press in the grain with their hooves.

AT HOME WITH HORI

Here you can see into Hori's house. As one of the scribes working on the pharaoh's tomb, Hori is a respected and wealthy official. The house is built of sun-dried mud bricks with wooden columns; only the doorways and column bases are made of stone. Leaving the house takes you into the bustle of one of the narrow streets of Deir el Medinah, the village especially built for the various skilled craftsmen working on the pharaoh's tombs.

Deir el Medinah was part of the city of Thebes, the religious center in southern Egypt. The main part of the city was on the east bank of the Nile, whereas the tombs, in the Valley of the Kings, and Deir el Medinah were on the west bank.

A Visit to Deir el Medinah
Neb's wife, Merit, is visiting her sister Tuya, who is married to the scribe Hori. Hori and Tuya hurry to welcome Merit into their house.

A village festival
Hori has been married before. His children are playing with friends on the roof. School is closed so that everyone can prepare for a festival tomorrow in honor of the founder of the village, Amenhotep I.

At the shrine
Tuya is going to have a baby. In ancient times, this could be dangerous. Tuya spends a lot of time praying at the house shrine dedicated to her ancestors and to the goddesses who help women, such as Isis.

Inside the house
The shrine is in the front room, which Hori also uses for his work. Honored guests like Merit are entertained in the central hall, which is higher than the other rooms, with the windows at ceiling level.

Life on the roof
Because the houses here are small, hot, and crowded, people go up to their roofs for the breeze. They put up awnings to shade them from the heat of the sun. In summer, they may even sleep on the roof.

Slave labor
There is no such thing as money yet so Hori is paid with goods or labor. As part of his wages, he is given wine, which he keeps in the cellar, and slaves who are sent to grind his grain.

A passion for paint
The walls of the main rooms are decorated, and all the wooden furniture is painted in bright colors. There are beds, tables, chairs, and stools, as well as boxes and baskets in which to store things.

Street life
The streets are narrow, dusty, and noisy. Goods and water from the Nile are carried to the village by donkey. Only the noblemen have chariots; everyone else walks. People buy their food from the small stalls.

THE SECRETS OF THE TOMB

The Egyptians worshiped many gods and goddesses who they believed took care of different parts of their lives. Neb lived during the New Kingdom (1567-1085 BC) and worshiped Amen-Re.

The Egyptians believed that a person's body remained on earth after death, but the soul, or spirit, left the body to enjoy an eternal life in the kingdom of the god Osiris, which was like a perfect Egypt.

1 The mourners
Members of Hori's family surround the dead man's bed. Although the family is there, professional mourners are also hired to follow the procession and show the family's respect for their dead relative.

2 Embalming
The embalmers remove the dead man's brain and internal organs, which are put to one side. They then pack a salt called *natron* around the body to dry it out, preserving it for the afterlife.

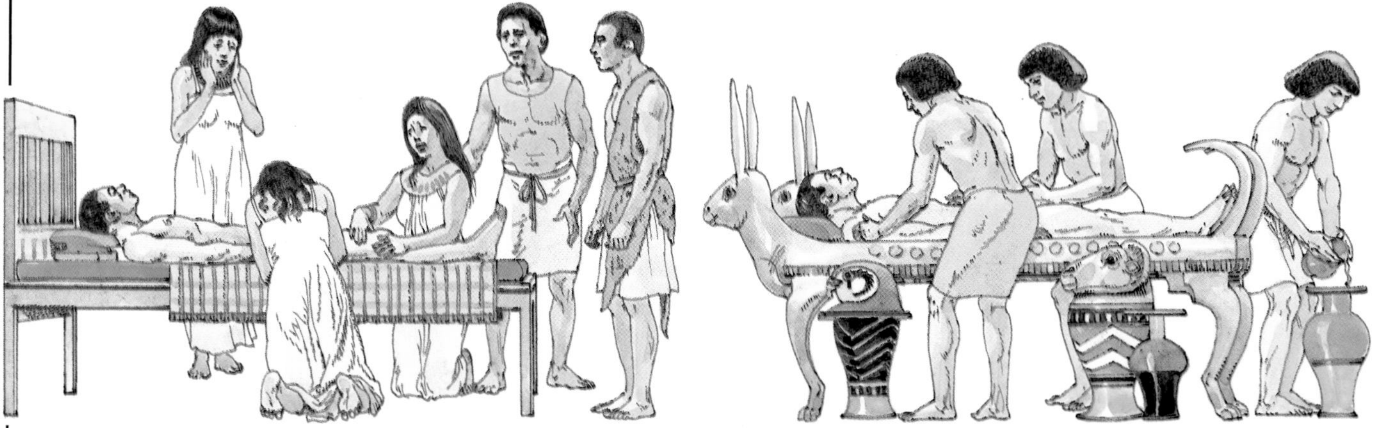

5 The procession
On the funeral day, relatives and servants carrying the dead man's possessions walk from his house to the embalmers' workshop. There they join the priest and hired mourners. The mummy, in its body-shaped coffin, is put on a sled. It is followed by the *canopic chest*, on another sled, which holds the internal organs.

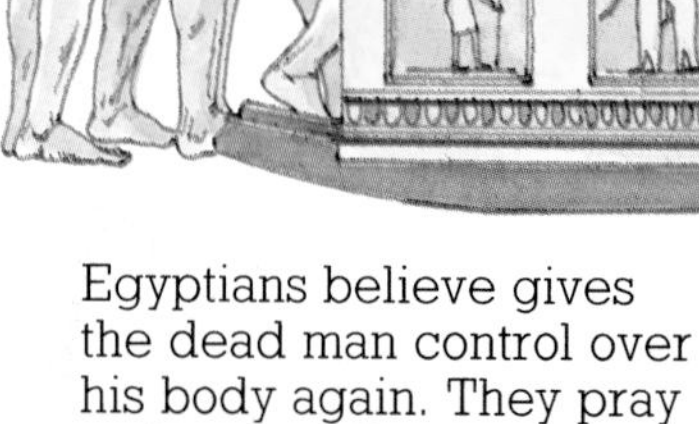

6 "Opening the mouth"
At the door of the tomb, a priest performs a rite called "Opening the Mouth," which the Egyptians believe gives the dead man control over his body again. They pray and make offerings.

7 The final farewell
They take the coffin down into the burial chamber and put it into a second, rectangular outer coffin, with a wreath of flowers. Farewells are said, and the lid is sealed.

The Egyptians believed that to enjoy eternal life, the body should be preserved and placed in a tomb with its possessions. Prayers and spells insured that the soul had an endless supply of food.

A life after death

Hori's brother has just died, so here you can see how the Egyptians preserve a body for the afterlife.

3 The mummy
They then wrap the body in many yards of linen. As they wind the layers around, they place jewelry and amulets, or charms, between the layers and pray for the man's soul.

4 Masks of the gods
On the mummy they place a mask that is a portrait of the dead man. The whole process takes 70 days, and during that time, the embalmers put on animal masks and act the roles of the gods.

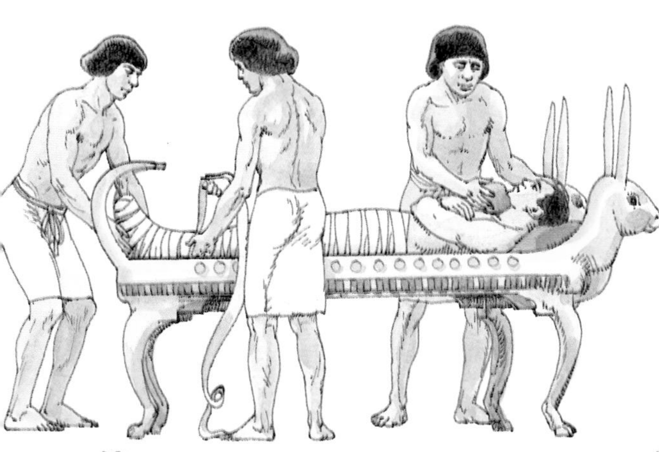

8 "Removing the Foot"
A priest sweeps the chamber where the coffin lies in the rite of "Removing the Foot." By removing any traces of human life, the Egyptians believe they can keep evil away from the tomb.

9 The Judgment Hall
After a feast, the funeral is over. The Egyptians believed the man's soul had by then arrived in the Judgment Hall of Osiris, to be weighed against a feather. If the two balance, it means he led a good life.

THE WEALTH OF THE SEA KING

It is still the same time, 1480 BC, but you have followed the Nile River north into the Mediterranean Sea, to arrive in the blazing sunshine on the rocky island of Crete.

The Cretans were farmers and sailors whose island had been free from invasion for centuries. As a result, the civilization that grew up was unique. They even developed their own way of writing,

The palace of Knossos

You are standing in the famous palace of Knossos. One of the girls who approaches the king, her brother, is Dictynna, princess of the royal house of Minos.

Royal duties
The princess is greeting ambassadors from Crete's great trading partner, the city of Byblos. They bring many gifts to honor Dictynna's brother, who has recently become king following the death of their father.

Bull leaping *(below)*

The visitors are most impressed by the bull leapers. These young men and women risk their lives by vaulting between the horns of charging bulls in the palace courtyard. It is done to honor the gods and for excitement. Artists use it as a theme for some of the rich *frescoes*, or wall paintings, that decorate the palace.

A stone goddess *(right)*

At her private shrine in the palace, Dictynna prays each day, making offerings of flowers, food, and wine. Following the fashion of the women attending court, the statuette of a goddess wears a flounced bell-shaped skirt beneath an open bodice, and her hair is arranged in long curls. In her hands she holds two vipers.

which is now called "Linear A." The Cretans were great builders and artisans who produced beautiful pottery and other goods, which they traded for metal and precious stones. They also produced grain, olives, fruit, and wine, which were stored in the palaces for export or payment to craftsmen. Crete was ruled from the palaces by a succession of kings, who reigned over the people.

Sea creatures
The Cretans love the sea, which gives them fish to eat and wealth from trade. This is shown in the lively fish and other sea creatures painted on their walls and pottery.

Clean living
Knossos has a complicated drainage system to carry away water from the spring and autumn rains. The Cretans consider cleanliness to be very important, and so the palaces are well supplied with bathrooms.

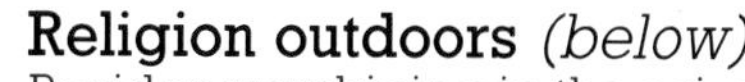

Religion outdoors *(below)*
Besides worshiping in the private shrines in palaces and houses, the Cretans also worshiped in caves and on mountainsides. This seal, used to stamp a design on clay or wax, shows a goddess with her priestesses and the sacred double axe.

Stored in jars *(above)*
When Knossos was excavated, archaeologists found a maze of large storerooms beneath the palace filled with many enormous jars that once held farm produce waiting to be traded.

INVADERS FROM THE NORTH

Gaul was the homeland of a fierce people called the Celts. They were farmers with a special interest in cattle and horses. They used iron for their weapons and tools, and wore trousers – strange to the people of the Mediterranean, but practical for horse-riding. With blaring battle trumpets and war paint, Celtic warriors were terrifying in battle.

The Celts were settled around Hallstatt, in modern Austria, by about 700 BC, where they prospered by mining and trading in precious salt. From this alpine region they spread westward through France and Spain, and northward into Holland and Britain. They also went south into Italy where they sacked the city of Rome in 385 BC, and the city of Delphi, in Greece, about a century later. As the Romans' empire expanded (see page 44), they slowly conquered all the Celtic lands, except for Ireland and parts of Scotland, but not without meeting resistance.

A family of metalworkers

Kai lives in a large village in central Gaul. Because his family have always been metalsmiths, they are highly respected by the tribe and have a large and well-equipped hut.

Fenced in
Kai's village belongs to the chief of the tribe, who controls the area. The tribe defends its village by encircling the timber and thatch huts with a tall wooden fence called a *palisade* and a deep ditch.

Raiders!
The tribe lives under constant threat from raiders, who steal cattle from the chief's territory. But the Celts are prepared; armed with spears and shields, they can pursue the raiders on foot or in horse-drawn chariots.

A fair description
The Greek writers describe the Celts as tall, fair, and keen to display their battle honors by wearing elaborate armor and weapons.

From power to plows
Below the chief and his family are the nobles, who are usually warriors; the *druids* (holy men); the artisans, and finally, the common people. Most Celts are farmers, and they use cattle to pull their special iron-tipped plows.

All dressed up
Using an iron cooking pot over the fire, Kai's mother helps prepare a feast to welcome some Greek traders from a colony in the south. To mark the event, they dress in brightly colored woolen clothes, woven in patterns.

Forging ahead

You have walked out of Kai's hut, and from where you stand you can see the metalsmiths hard at work. Kai's ancestors were among the first people to extract ore from rocks by using great heat, and to mix different metals to produce bronze. He is proud of his family history and longs to be as skilled as his father.

Emergency builders

The hut belonging to Kai's uncle was destroyed by a fire. the villagers help to rebuild it. Men on the ground prepare mud for the walls, and a couple are binding together bundles of straw to be fixed into the wooden framework of the roof.

Men of iron

Not only do the Celts use iron to make tools and weapons, but they also use gold and bronze to make fine jewelry, decorative armor, and containers. All of these beautiful items are highly valued for trade.

A gift to the goddess

After an attack, the Celts gather up the enemy's armor and give it to a druid. Adding some new pieces, made by Kai's family, the druid throws it into the river. This offering thanks the tribe's mother goddess for victory.

Fear of attack

Kai envies the warriors who triumphantly return from battle boasting of their deeds. But in spite of their victories, the chief knows that the village needs better protection than a fence. He wants to build a hill fort for the tribe.

How we know

Due to decay there are very few ordinary objects, such as baskets, leatherwork and cloth, for us to study. Much of our knowledge about Celtic society comes from surviving Celtic legends and languages, such as Welsh and Gaelic, and from place names. Also, impressive hill forts have been excavated. Their earthworks, great excavations of land surrounding a fortified village, look like huge steps cut into a hill.

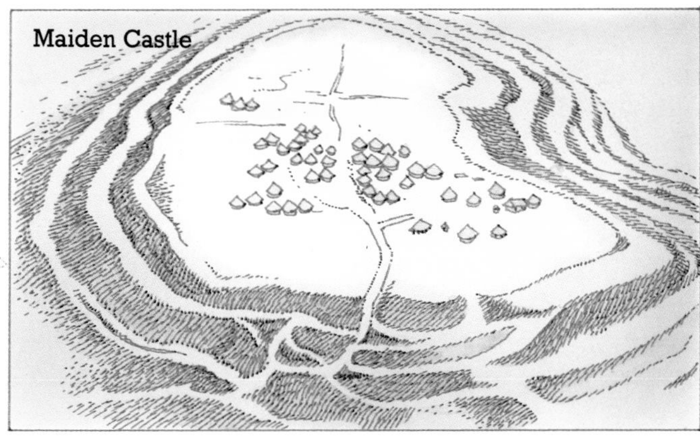

Armed to the teeth

Long swords, daggers, and spears are the warriors' favorite weapons. Their bravery, coupled with the strength of their new iron weapons, makes them frightening opponents. The men also use slings as weapons. Apart from armor for battle, they also have magnificently decorated pieces for display only, as well as excellent tools.

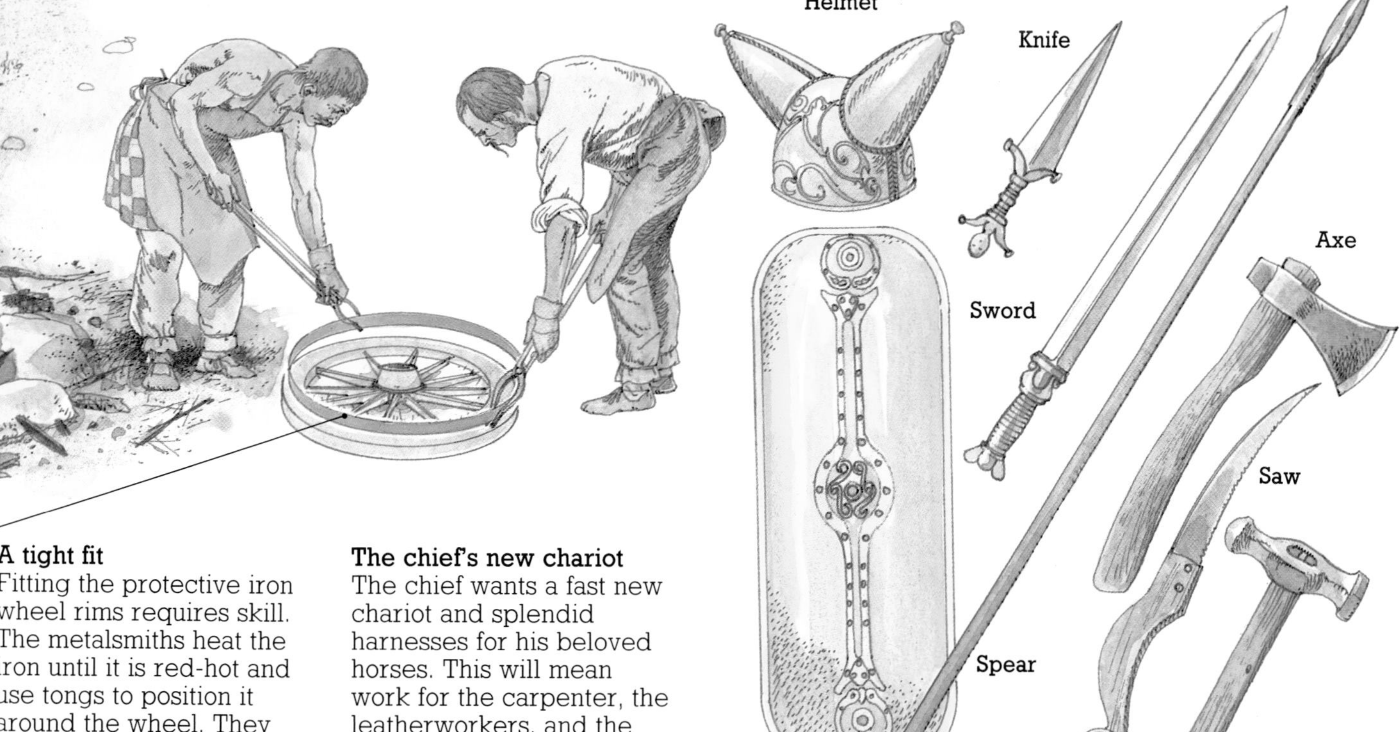

A tight fit

Fitting the protective iron wheel rims requires skill. The metalsmiths heat the iron until it is red-hot and use tongs to position it around the wheel. They then pour water over the iron; as it cools, it shrinks into place.

The chief's new chariot

The chief wants a fast new chariot and splendid harnesses for his beloved horses. This will mean work for the carpenter, the leatherworkers, and the village smiths. Chariots are made of wood, but the wheel rims are iron.

HERDSMEN OF SIBERIA

From Gaul, you have traveled thousands of miles east to an area that is now called Siberia. The date is 500 BC, and for miles around are the vast expanses of treeless plains and snowcapped mountains now known as the steppes.

The tribes that lived in the harsh conditions of Siberia were nomadic, constantly moving their families and animals in search of new pastures.

Rather than hunting the wild horses that lived on the steppes for meat, these nomadic tribes caught and tamed them. They then rode the horses at great speed, rounding up other wild horses, which they sold or used for carrying loads and providing milk.

The horsemen were frightening warriors. They were highly skilled archers and greatly feared by the Chinese, Persians, and Greeks, who also noted their excellence with horses. The nomadic metalsmiths produced fine ornaments, and the women made intricately sewn designs.

Away from home
At certain times of the year, the men round up the wild horses and herd them to distant pastures where the grazing is better. The herdsmen sleep in felt or birch-bark tents when they are far from home.

Food and fodder
The herdsmen hunt wild deer for meat, but they also breed sheep, some cattle, and chickens. The only crop is hay, which they store to feed the animals during the winter.

The horsemen of the Altai Mountains
You have joined a tribe of herdsmen from the west of Siberia. Rudek, the chief, and his men have herded the horses back home.

Horseplay
The tribesmen are proud of their horses. On special occasions, Rudek puts on his horse a brightly embroidered saddle, plaits its tail, and fits to its head decorations that look like reindeer antlers.

Settling down
When the herdsmen return, they join their families in a settlement of houses made of logs, with bark roofs. Inside, the women make *appliqués* by sewing shapes of material onto a background.

Making leather

How we know

These people had no written language, so much of our knowledge about them comes from tombs discovered at Pazyryk in the steppes. Individuals were buried deep in a log-lined pit covered with stones. With them were their horses and possessions. A few years later, the tombs were broken open by robbers, allowing water to seep in. The water then froze, preserving what remained in the tombs.

Skin-deep
The tribesmen's clothes are made of linen, wool, fur, and leather, to keep them warm. They love lavish embroidery and golden ornaments. Rudek has *tattoos*, like drawings, stained into his skin.

Pots and pans
The tribesmen have low wooden tables with oval tops and carved legs, and sit on stools or cushions. Stone oil lamps provide light. They use leather, clay and wooden bowls, and copper caldrons.

LIFE IN ANCIENT GREECE

So little is known about what happened in Greece in the years 1000-800 BC that the period is called the Greek Dark Ages. But now it is about 424 BC, and you have arrived in the magnificent city of Athens.

In the 400 years or so after the Dark Ages, Greece grew into one of the greatest civilizations in history. It produced some of the best playwrights and philosophers, or thinkers, ever known, and the *classical* style of its architecture and statues was copied for many centuries.

Lysander

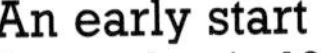

An early start
Lysander is 12 years old. This year his father is a city official, chosen by fellow citizens. Because Amyntas is wealthy, he has been able to pay for Lysander to go to school from the earliest age, 7 years old. A slave helps Lysander get dressed.

Plans over breakfast
Lysander has a quick breakfast of bread, cheese, and olives. He plans to sneak off to see his father speak at the assembly of citizens, which meets three or four times a month. Today, they will be discussing new peace proposals for the states.

Family prayers
Every day, before leaving the house, the family meets for prayers around the altar in the courtyard. Today, Philip, Lysander's elder brother, is setting out to fight in the wars between Athens and Sparta, so they ask the goddess Athena for help.

Thea

Getting dressed
Thea, Lysander's 10-year-old sister, is washing under a waterspout in the villa before dressing. She normally wears a *chiton*, a simple robe made of a piece of linen (or wool in winter) sewn together down the side, but left open at the top.

Homework
Like other girls, Thea does not go to school. Instead, her mother teaches her the skills expected of a wife, in preparation for when she is married. By that time, she must be able to run a large household, and organize the slaves, and manage the food bills.

Going out
Because she comes from a good family, Thea spends most of her time at home. She occasionally visits friends and accompanies her mother to the temples on festival days. Each temple is dedicated to one of the many Greek gods and goddesses.

Ancient Greece was divided into city-states, and rivalries developed between the strong states, particularly Athens and Sparta. Each state had its own rulers, but Athens had a *democracy*, where the citizens elected their leaders. All freemen were citizens, but women, children, and slaves, were not.

Just an ordinary day

Lysander, Alexander, and Thea are the children of Amyntas and Campaspne. Here you can see how they spend a typical day in their hometown, Athens.

Waxworks
Lysander has his own slave, who takes him to school and stays with him to make sure he works. The boys write with a pointed *stylus* on wooden tablets covered with wax. When the tablets are full, they smooth over the wax and start again.

Early adding machines
To help with his sums, each pupil has an *abacus*. This is a wooden frame that has wires strung across it, threaded with beads. The boys study many subjects: the works of the famous Greek poets and playwrights, music, and history.

Budding athletes
Athletics takes up part of each day. Lysander practices running, jumping, boxing, and wrestling. He excels at throwing the *discus* (a plate-shaped piece of copper) and the spear-shaped javelin. Every four years, he visits the Olympic games.

Alexander

Discussion group
Alexander is the second son of the family. He is 17 and left school two years ago. Now he is attending classes on public speaking and takes part in discussion groups conducted by one of the city's leading philosophers.

The theater
Alexander is stagestruck. After seeing a play by Euripides, he wants to write his own play. The theaters are open-air, and audiences sit in seats cut out of a hillside in a circular arrangment around the stage. The actors, all men, wear masks.

Military training
Next year, Alexander will come of age and be considered a citizen. All young men are taught from boyhood to be soldiers, and Alexander must do two years' military service. He practices with a sword, shield, and spear.

LYSANDER'S HOME

It is early evening of the following day, and you are in the family's large house in Athens.

Paintings, statues, and *relief sculptures* (pictures carved or modeled out of the surface of a flat piece of stone or clay) give us a clue about how the Greeks lived at home. Most large houses in Athens were built of sun-dried bricks on a carefully leveled stone base. The wood-frame roof was covered with overlapping tiles. The public rooms and kitchen were on the ground floor, with the private quarters and bedrooms above. At the center of the house was a courtyard, in which stood the family altar. A wooden staircase led from the courtyard to the upper story. Wealthy families had wells, but most people fetched water in large pottery jars from public fountains.

Night lights
In the bedroom, a slave is putting a chiton into the storage chest. Behind her are wooden couches with covers and pillows for sleeping on, and a tall holder for an oil lamp.

The dinner party
Amyntas is giving a dinner party for friends because he wants to talk about business. The guests lie on couches, eating from a low table. The women never join the men to eat.

Home furnishings
The furniture is wooden or bronze, sometimes inlaid with precious metals and ivory. Athenians also have folding leather stools and chairs. They keep clothes in large baskets or chests.

The altar
The Greeks believe in many gods and goddesses, and over the years they have built up myths around them. The father of the gods is Zeus, who lives on Mount Olympus.

A full house
Lysander's family is scattered throughout the house. it is early evening, and the slaves are preparing food in the kitchen or weaving cloth in the room above it. The noisiest place is the room rented by the potter.

How we know
We get a lot of information about everyday life from the paintings on Greek pottery. There are two famous kinds of pottery – black-figured ware and red-figured ware. Both often showed scenes of domestic life.

The heart of the house
The courtyard is always busy. Campaspne protects herself from the sun while she sits with her children. A messenger arrives with news from Philip: Athens has been defeated.

Women's work
Several slaves have been bought for their spinning and weaving skills. In addition to making woolen and linen cloth for the family's clothes, they weave wall hangings.

A slave's freedom
The slaves are cooking meat and vegetables over a charcoal fire. They bake the bread in ovens. Household slaves earn tips and some save enough to buy their freedom.

Pots of money
Amyntas owns several farms, and he makes money from selling the farm produce. But recently he has been unable to pay the high taxes, so he rents a room to a potter.

MARKET DAY IN ATHENS

A few days have passed, and you have walked a short distance from Lysander's house, through the crowded streets to the marketplace, or *agora*.

In Athens, as in other Greek cities, some craftsmen sold their wares directly from their workshops, but most people did their shopping in the agora. Merchants set up stalls in the open area of the agora and under the shade of the *stoa*. This was a long, two-story building. One side of it was open and supported by columns. The citizens went there to buy goods and slaves, and to hire workers. They also used it as a meeting place. Men often did the shopping; if they were rich, they took slaves along to carry the purchases. In Athens, officials checked the quality of the goods and ensured that the sellers used accurate scales and measures.

Shopping around
The owners of the market stalls are busy trading. All around you, goods and money are changing hands and people are exchanging ideas and gossip.

Banking
Because everyone now uses money, banks are necessary. In the market-pace, bankers will lend money to most people. But like the money changers, they charge a fee.

Oil for washing
Everyone buys olive oil for cooking. They also burn it in lamps and use it instead of soap, rubbing it over their bodies and then scraping it off, along with the dirt.

An expensive butcher
Farmers breed goats, pigs, chickens, and less often, sheep for meat. They sell it in the market, but only the rich can afford meat. Most people eat fish, eggs, fruit, and vegetables.

Choosing fabrics
Most people buy material in the market. They usually choose plain linen or wool, and save brightly colored clothes for very special occasions. The Greeks also import silk from the East.

How we know
Today we have many Greek coins to study. The most common shape is a circle of metal with a symbol, or picture, of the city's chief god or goddess. Later coins are stamped with the portraits of city rulers.

From barter to money
Instead of bartering, the Greeks use pieces of metal stamped by the city officials as a guarantee of their value. Such coins were invented around 600 BC in the Greek colony of Lydia, in Turkey.

Money changing
Because each city has its own coinage, people have to exchange their money when visiting another city before spending any money there. Money changers in the agora charge a fee for this service.

A sweet tooth
Lysander tries to persuade Amyntas to buy something sweet. The Greeks do not have sugar, so they sweeten their food with honey. The beekeepers use special pottery hives.

The tavern
Alexander spends a lot of his time drinking wine with friends in the *taverna*, a popular meeting place for men. The wine, made from local grapes, is stored in pottery jars.

A VISIT TO CHINA

You have traveled east for thousands of miles and have arrived in China. It is around 130 BC, and the Han dynasty, or family of rulers, is in power.

An independent and major civilization grew up in the huge country of China. Its great cities produced inventive artisans and ingenious writers and thinkers. The Chinese established carefully ordered societies that deeply honored their ancestors.

As early as 5000 BC, the people farmed millet and soy beans and later rice, and bred dogs and pigs. They also raised silkworms, having discovered that these caterpillars produce a thread that can be woven into fine cloth. After 1500 BC, during the Shang dynasty, they created a system of writing and invented a method for casting bronze. Following two centuries of civil war, the country united under the emperor of Ch'in, the dynasty that gave China its name. The Ch'in emperors began major work on the massive Great Wall, built to defend the northern border. In 206 BC, the Han dynasty seized power.

The Lady Ch'eng

These pages show the palace of Lady Ch'eng, wife of the Han emperor Ching, just before she gets sick and dies.

Home sweet home

The people's houses are wooden and the thin walls are painted with lacquer to waterproof them. Often the houses have two stories and are topped with watchtowers so that a lookout can give an early warning of any attack.

How we know

When Lady Ch'eng dies, her tomb is sealed with thick layers of clay and charcoal to preserve these items.

A box of cosmetics

Perfectly preserved in the tomb is a box painted with lacquer, a glossy paint made from tree sap. A silk scarf and mittens are in the top of the box, and in a number of smaller boxes below are brushes, combs, and cosmetics.

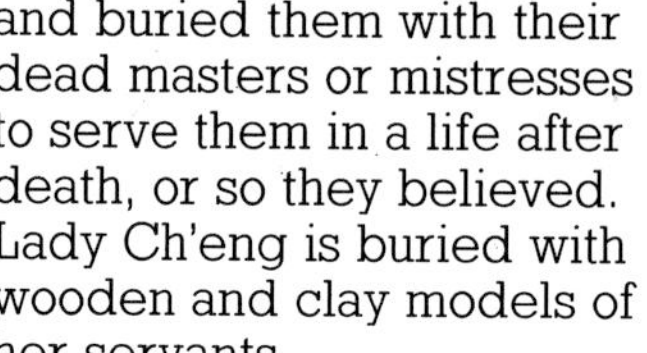

Servants for eternity

In earlier dynasties, the Chinese killed servants and buried them with their dead masters or mistresses to serve them in a life after death, or so they believed. Lady Ch'eng is buried with wooden and clay models of her servants.

Bitter medicines
Lady Ch'eng is about 50 years old. She wears a hairpiece. In recent years, she has had problems with a weak heart. Her doctors have prescribed various medicines, including cinnamon, peppercorns, and ground magnolia bark.

A gift horse
Lady Ch'eng rests by the pool as she waits to see a horse that the emperor has given one of their sons. It was brought from the West, and is larger and swifter than Chinese horses. Only the rich have horses and carriages for traveling in.

A painted palace
The palace, also wooden, has several stories. Its inside is richly decorated with paintings and finely worked bronze ornaments. The beautiful grounds that surround the palace contain decorative ponds and an ornamental house.

Miniature houses
Tombs often contain models of houses, made of intricately worked bronze or pottery. Some of these have their own courtyards complete with wells; some are farmhouses with model animals and granaries for storage.

Covered in silk
Silk garments are buried with Lady Ch'eng. One dress is so fine that it weighs almost nothing. Her shoes, stockings, and mittens are also silk. Some items are plain, but others are decorated with paint and embroidery.

ROMAN FAMILY LIFE

You have traveled far to the west again, back to Europe. Your new location is a boot-shaped country called Italy. It is about 20 BC, and you are in the countryside around ancient Rome. Rome grew into one of the most successful empires in history from a settlement around the Tiber River. At the height of its power, it controlled the whole of Italy and vast areas of land that extended

Caius Claudius Sabinus
On these pages, you can see into the villa, or country house, belonging to Claudius, a wealthy senator.

Heated floors
At the center of the villa is an *atrium*, or open-air courtyard. All the rooms in the front open off the atrium. A pool in the middle catches valuable rainwater. Under the house is a central heating system called a *hypocaust.*

Painted walls
The walls are decorated with frescoes, or wall paintings, as in Crete, and the ground floor is paved with marble. Claudius wants a *mosaic* floor, made from tiny pieces of inlaid stone, and he also wants to buy a new marble statue.

Reflected glory
Bedrooms are on the second floor. Paulina is the wife of Claudius's son Marcus. A slave arranges her hair in fashionable curls while she is shown the result in a silver mirror. Her fine jewelry is made of gold and precious gems.

Matchmaking
Julia, Claudius's wife, is seated on a couch, talking to Senator Vitellius and his wife, Tullia. They are planning a marriage between their son, who is in the army, and Julia's daughter. The young couple talk in the atrium.

north into England and south into Egypt.

Rome was a *republic*, a form of government headed by representatives elected by the citizens. The Roman republic was ruled by two consuls, who were advised by the senators, a group of men chosen from leading Roman families. But in 27 BC, a man called Octavian seized power becoming the first emperor of Rome, calling himself Augustus.

School time
Because Claudius is rich, he does not send his son Julius to school, but employs a Greek former slave as tutor. Girls rarely attend lessons, but today Livia has joined her brother as the teacher reads from a scroll of papyrus, or *volumen*.

The eldest son
Claudius is in the study with Marcus, his eldest son. Octavian, now Emperor Augustus, likes Claudius, so he is optimistic about his son's career. Marcus has had good training as a *tribune*, or officer, in the army.

THE JOURNEY BACK TO ROME

You have joined Claudius and his family as they return to their town house in Rome. The new road stretches in a straight line toward the city.

As Rome expanded its empire, armies needed to move farther and faster. Thousands of miles of roads were built to help the men move more quickly. In 146 BC, after many years of fighting, the Roman army conquered Greece. The Romans learned a great deal from the Greeks and adopted many of their ideas. They copied Greek art and architecture and used Greek engineering skills in warfare and building. The Romans added to these skills by inventing a strong concretelike building material made from the volcanic rock *tufa*. This allowed them to build more daring structures, such as arches.

All roads lead to Rome
These pages show how Claudius's family travels. They usually take an armed escort because bandits sometimes attack and rob travelers.

Building bridges
Slaves, who do the building in Rome, are constructing arches around a wooden framework. They will remove the framework once the bridge is secure. They use wooden cranes to lift the building stones.

Family travel
The women travel in *litters*, which are like carriages without wheels, carried by slaves. Marcus takes Julius in his chariot, and Claudius rides his favorite horse. They pass carriages, carts, and wagons, as well as people on foot.

Long-distance water
The Romans use a lot of water, which they often have to bring from miles away. For this they build water-carrying bridges, or *aqueducts.*

Foot soldiers
These soldiers are heading back to headquarters in the city. While extending its empire, Rome is frequently at war, and so has built up a highly efficient army.

By the wayside
In remote areas, travelers have to set up camp for the night. But along main roads, there are plenty of wayside inns where people can eat, sleep, and hire fresh horses. Claudius prefers his family to stay with friends on the way.

Building the road
The slaves dig a trench, put curbstones along the sides and then fill the trench will layers of sand and pebbles. The top layer is made of shaped stones. The surface is slightly curved so water drains off. The surveyor uses an instrument called a *grommeticus* to check the level.

A ROMAN STREET SCENE

Before going to Claudius's house, you stop in a much poorer part of Rome, where the tradesmen, artisans, and less prosperous people live.

Most Romans did not come from rich families, and although all men were citizens (excluding slaves and foreigners), few had much money and most lived in badly built, wood-framed apartments above shops. There were not enough jobs, so Roman officials distributed free grain to the unemployed, built splendid public bathhouses, and arranged spectator sports and chariot races to amuse the public.

The street life
Here you can see the people and houses in the poorer part of Rome. Marcus's new job is to collect taxes from them.

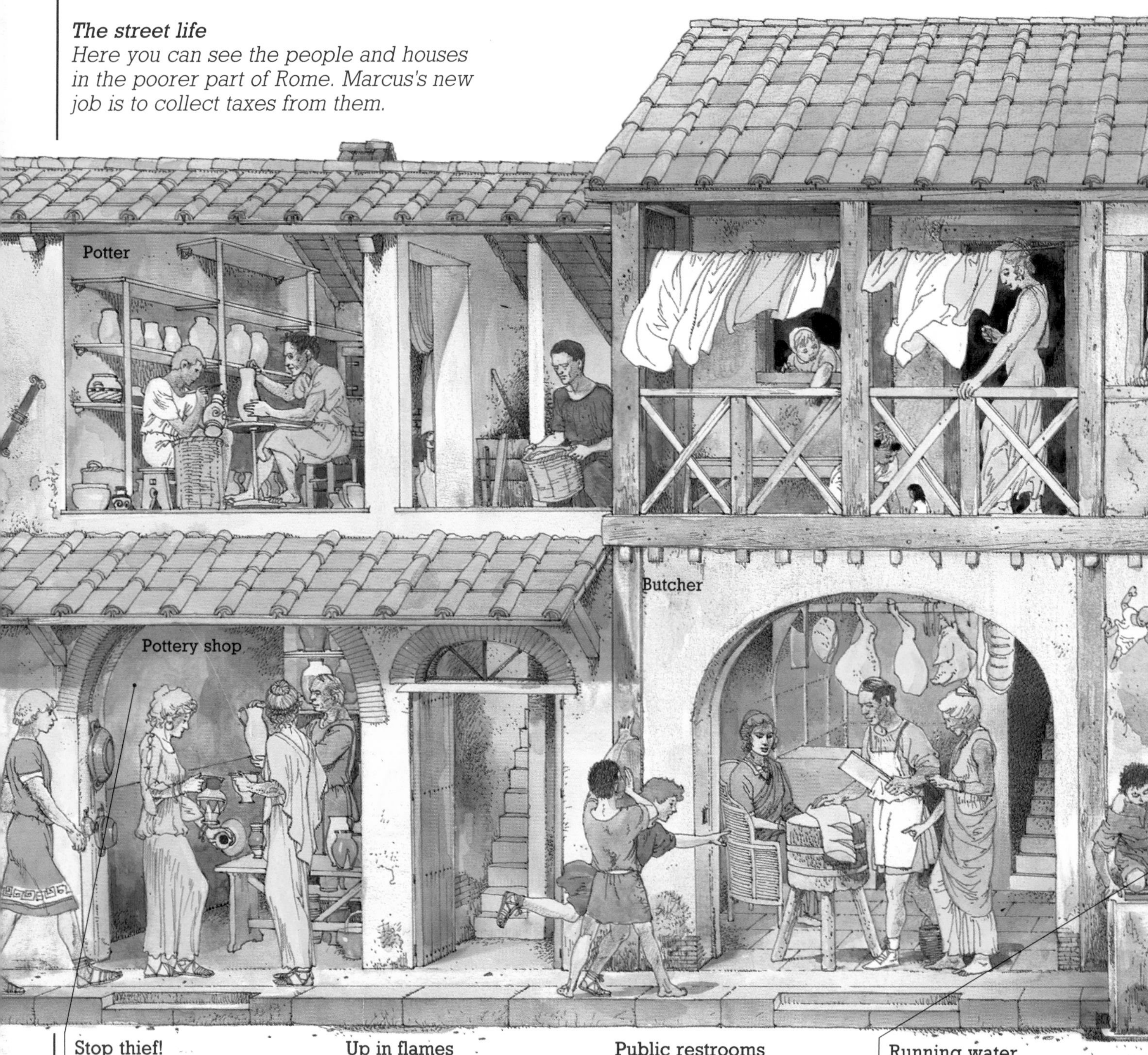

Stop thief!
The shops are open to the pavement and have their counters at the front. At night, the tradesmen fit wooden shutters across the shops and lock them to discourage thieves.

Up in flames
In the poorer parts of the city, the overcrowded buildings sometimes fall down, killing the people inside. Fires are common, so there are watchmen and a fire-fighting force.

Public restrooms
The more expensive, ground-floor apartments have private bathrooms connected to the main sewers. But most people use the public facilities located on every street.

Running water
Most apartment-dwellers get their drinking water from the stone public fountains on every street. They have to pay officials to have water piped directly into their homes.

Rooms for rent
Very few people can afford houses; most live in apartment blocks and rent one or more rooms. A few apartments are comfortable, but most are in need of repair.

Shops
The apartments are built around small courtyards, and many people rent out their front rooms to businesses like potters and barbers. Many people also work in the courtyards.

Food and drink
Few of the apartments have kitchens, so most people buy cooked food. There are bakeries that sell olive oil, wine, and hot food. Vegetables are sold in the market.

The sewers
Clay sewage pipes run from the bathrooms to a system of pipes under the sidewalks. These pipes then join the main tunnels that carry all the waste into the Tiber River.

A DAY WITH CLAUDIUS

You have left the poorer area of Rome to rejoin Senator Claudius for a day mixing pleasure with work.

Senators came from a group of people at the top of Roman society. Beneath them were the *equites*, successful men involved in business. The largest group of people were the poorest, the *plebeians*. Every freeman was a citizen and could wear a *toga*, a large piece of cloth wrapped around the body, as a symbol of his citizenship. Women were in a weak

1 The family shrine
Every morning, Claudius leads the prayers as the whole family gathers around the shrine in the atrium. The shrine holds figures of the *lares* and *penates*, the guardian spirits of the house and family. The family also prays to Vesta, goddess of the hearth, who protects the household. Julia is faithful to the Egyptian goddess Isis.

2 Public baths
Although he has a perfectly good suite of baths in his town house, Claudius often chooses to go to the public bathhouse because he can meet friends and do business with colleagues. Today, he takes Marcus along. After leaving their clothes in the changing room, they sit in the "hot room," where boiling water gives off steam to make them sweat.

5 The library
Claudius goes home to his library. He should be preparing his speech for the next meeting of the Senate, but a bookseller has just delivered a copy of a new work on philosophy, and he cannot resist starting it. The book is a series of scrolls made of Egyptian papyrus. Like all Roman books, it was hand-copied, probably by a Greek slave.

6 The Senate
Claudius makes a point of attending every meeting of the Senate, even though the Senate has less control of Roman affairs, since the emperor seized power. Today, it is meeting to investigate the case of one of its own members who commands one of the provinces, a large area held by the empire. He has been accused of overtaxing the people.

position; the men in their family – whether the husband, father, or son – had authority over them, although divorce was possible. Finally there was a mass of slaves, captured as Rome extended its empire. A rich man might have 100 slaves.

Business and pleasure

Here you can see that Claudius has a full day. But between attending to his business and his duties as senator, he finds time to enjoy life.

3 A dip in the pool
Claudius and Marcus next pass through the hot- and warm-water baths, and finally swim in the cold water pool. They talk to friends and later have a light meal. Women have their own set of rooms at the bathhouses. A good bathhouse offers food, barbers, beauty treatments, a garden, a library, and an area for athletic exercise.

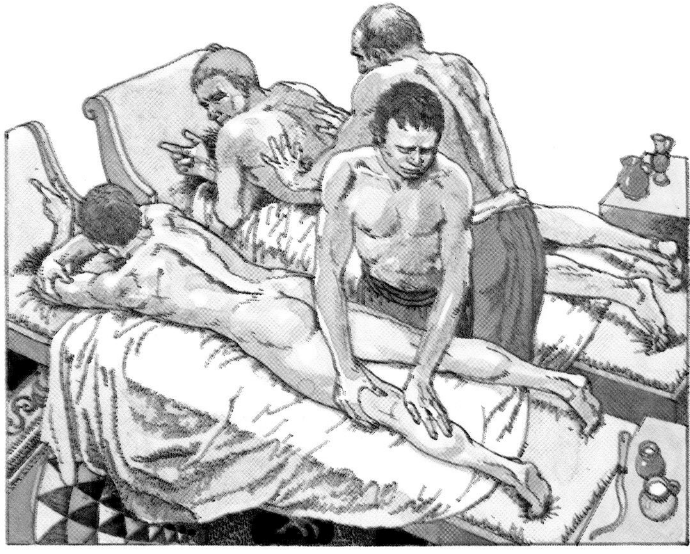

4 Secret worries
After bathing, Claudius and Marcus have a massage. It is a good opportunity to talk, but Marcus is silent. He is worried about money. His wife, Paulina, has gone in her litter to the forum, Rome's marketplace, where she wants to buy some oriental silk. Marcus is already in debt from betting on the chariot races and playing dice.

7 Bloodthirsty sports
Games are held in honor of the emperor's birthday, and huge crowds of Romans go to the coliseum, a massive theater without a stage, where the games are held. Most Romans are excited by watching the *gladiators*, prisoners who are trained to fight to the death. But Julia does not enjoy it and leaves before the rest of the crowd.

8 The dinner party
In the evening, Claudius and Julia give a party to celebrate the emperor's birthday. The guests lie on couches, helping themselves to the food with spoons and their fingers. The dishes include such delicacies as stuffed dormice, roast ostrich, and exotic fruits, washed down with wine drunk from glass goblets. Poets and musicians entertain.

AT HOME WITH THE VIKINGS

You have left the luxuries of Rome behind you, traveled north through what are now Switzerland and Germany, and crossed the icy North Sea into Norway. The journey has carried you forward in time to AD 950. In the meantime, the Roman Empire has collapsed and Christianity has spread to Europe.

Like Sweden, Denmark, and parts of Finland, the land we now know as Norway was populated by the Norsemen, a hardy people who engaged in farming, trade, and fishing. But they were better known as warriors and adventurers. By the end of the eighth century AD, the Norsemen had set out in sturdy boats and reached many parts of central Europe, where they looted, destroyed, and killed. Monks described the raiders' bloodstained progress in *chronicles* (like diaries), rulers offered rich payments in return for safety, and everyone prayed to be delivered from the Norsemen, whom they called Vikings.

The village of Eric the blacksmith
On these pages, you can discover a Viking village situated at the end of a fjord (a long inlet from the sea), where Eric is the chief's blacksmith.

Many farmhands
Eric works for the chief, Gorm One-Eye. Gorm, the members of his large family, and their followers farm the land, but a lot of the work is done by slaves, who were captured in a recent raid abroad.

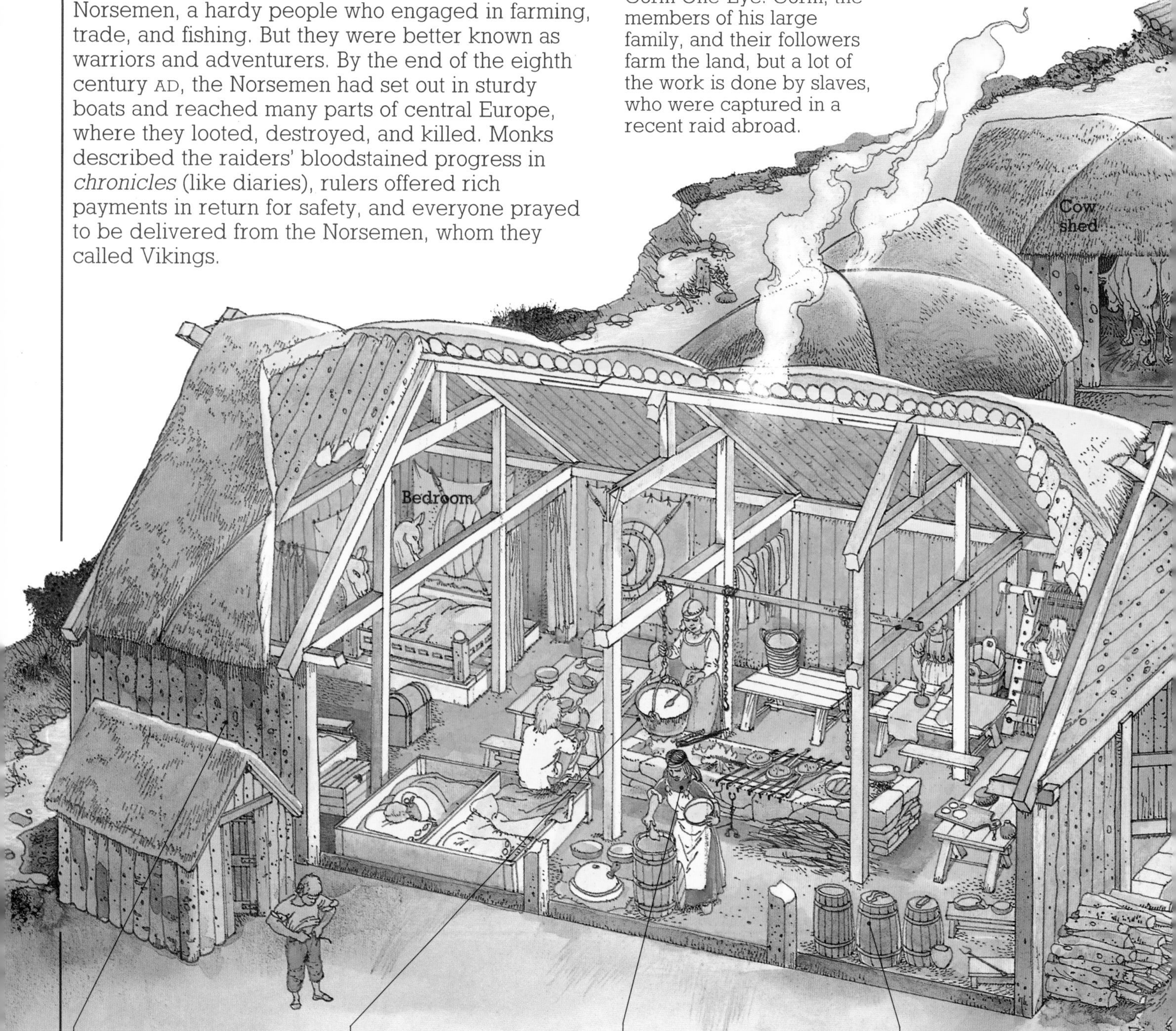

Houses like barns
A forest stretches between the village and the distant mountains, so timber is plentiful. The houses are timber-framed with wooden or stone walls, and the roofs are thatched.

A lack of privacy
The houses usually have a single windowless room in which everybody sleeps and eats. The women cook on a central hearth, and smoke escapes through a hole in the roof.

Surviving the winter
The villagers have to store food indoors to last all winter. They cannot feed all their animals during the winter, so they kill some and smoke and salt the meat to preserve it.

No spare room
Even in the summer, the houses are full of flour and other food stored in large barrels. The rest of the space is taken up with wooden beds and benches.

Weapons for warriors
Gorm respects Eric for his skill with bronze and iron. He makes excellent double-sided swords and flat blades with curved edges for the *broadaxes* used by the warriors.

A choice of food
The grain crop is vital because the people make it into bread, beer, and porridge. They grow vegetables and gather fruit and honey. But they have to trade for supplies of salt.

Fish and fowl
The Vikings breed cattle, sheep, goats, and pigs to provide them with meat, milk, wool, and leather. They raise chickens and geese. They also hunt for meat and catch fish.

Wandering seamen

You have now walked to the harbor, where people are loading one ship and building another.

The Vikings are inspired shipbuilders. Using local timber, usually oak, they build knorrs, *sturdy boats for fishing trips or local trading, and* longships, *warships used for raiding. By following the sun, stars, and any landmarks, they navigate across vast expanses of sea.*

Warrior-turned-trader

Since Gorm lost an eye, he concentrates on trading. The villagers load up one of the knorrs with farm produce and some metalwork for trade.

All hands on deck

The Viking ships can sail on rivers or on the sea. There is an oar-shaped wooden rudder for steering and a large square sail, but the men often row into and out of harbor.

Ship-shape
The shipbuilders create the boat's curved outline by first soaking the wood to make it pliable. The *keel*, a wooden strip attached to the underside of the boat, gives it stability.

How we know

Archaeological remains and written chronicles help us imagine the Vikings' way of life. The Viking tradition of burying their warriors in ships under a mound of earth means that there are marvelous remains to study today. Such ships have been found in Gokstad and Oseberg, in Norway. Also, five other ships, sunk by the Vikings to block a channel in the Norwegian Roskilde Fjord, have been preserved in mud.

Favorite ports
Gorm and his men often sail to Dublin, an Irish port, or to Sweden. In the great Swedish port of Birka, there are visiting Arabs eager to trade for furs, slaves, and precious lumps of amber.

Beastly carvings
Viking carvings in wood and stone often depict animals or intricate patterns. The artisans carve swirls or the heads of beasts on the front extensions, or *prows*, of their longships.

Viking boathouses
The villagers have small row boats in which they catch fish from the fjords, or even compete in rowing races for pleasure. When not in use, the boats are kept in thatched shelters.

A god of thunder
The Vikings worship many gods and goddesses. The father of their gods is Odin, god of wisdom and battle. They also place great faith in Thor, who rules the weather.

MEDIEVAL ENGLAND

After a voyage south, you find yourself in a small English village in about AD 1320. You have arrived during the Middle Ages, also called the medieval period, which lasted from around AD 1000 to 1450.

When William the Conqueror invaded England in AD 1066, he introduced a way of organizing the people that had developed in his homeland, in what is now France. This system was known as *feudalism*, and it worked liked this: the English king gave his nobles large areas of land in return for an oath of loyalty and a number of soldiers; the nobles allowed knights to use the land, and as payment, the knights offered to serve as soldiers required by the king. The peasants living on the knights' lands (*manors*), worked for their overlords, the knights, in return for protection.

Within four walls
Here you can see inside the house belonging to Agnes and Fulk. It looks rather crowded, but compared to many other peasants, they are fortunate.

Hardworking peasants
Some peasants are *freemen*, who pay only rent for their land; but most are *villeins* like Fulk. This means they have to pay money to their overlord, usually a knight, and work on his private land.

A cozy household
Fulk's house has a timber frame and walls made from a mixture of earth, clay, and straw. The roof is thatched, and there are wooden floorboards. The windows have no glass so they are shuttered at night.

Pork and porridge
The peasants wear linen or woolen clothes made from local material. They eat bread, porridge, and home-grown vegetables, but have pork and bacon on special occasions. Their cow provides the milk.

The animals next door
Most houses have one room for the family and another for the animals. Agnes and Fulk also have a separate parlor. They fill any available space with food, which has to last until the next harvest.

Little freedom
Villeins are tied to the land and can leave only if their overlord gives permission. They must work on his land, use his mill, and pay him *dues*, or fees, if they want to marry. As a result, they are poor.

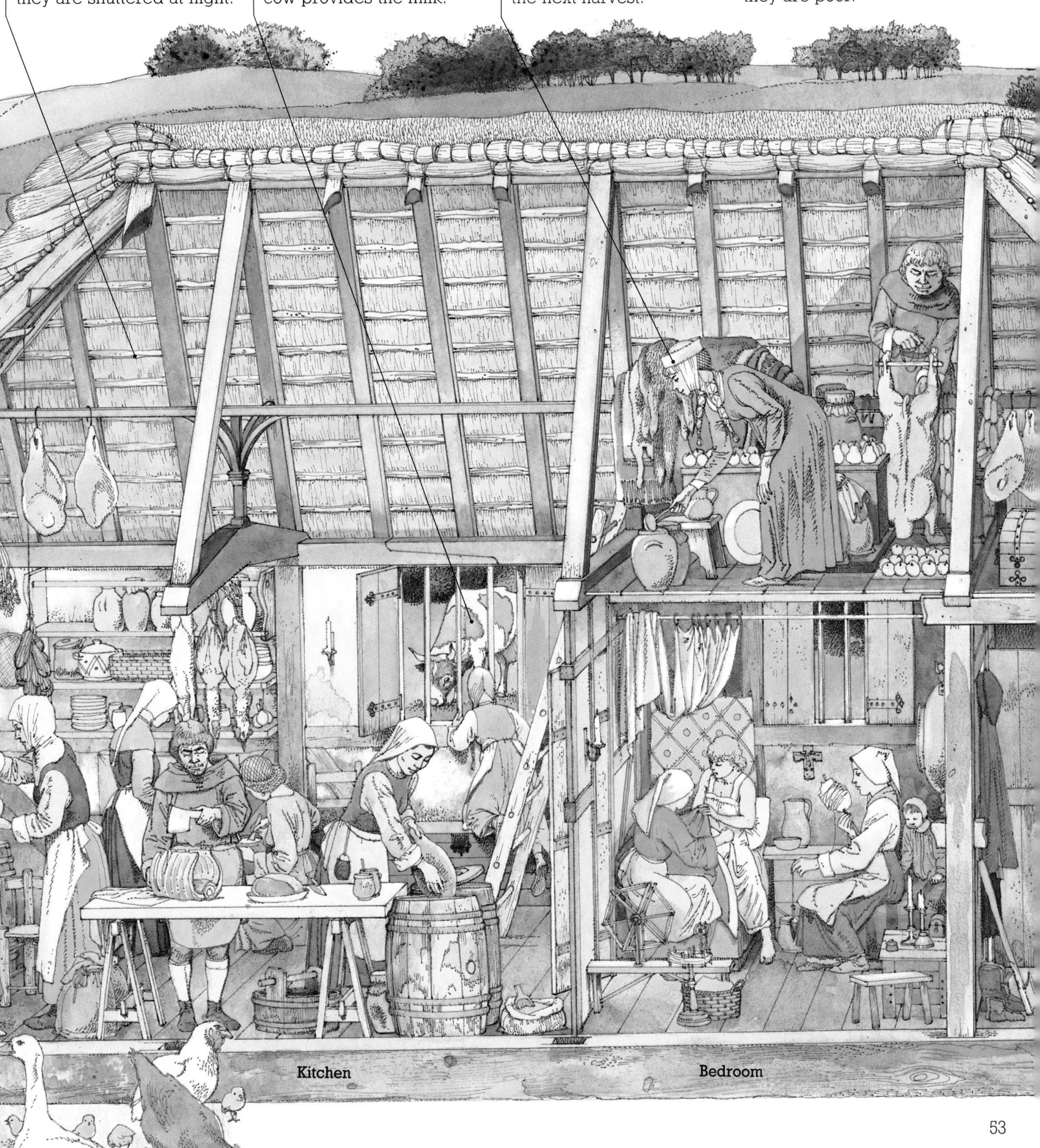

A growing village

The village is the center of the manor and answers most of the people's needs, but its wealth depends on the produce from the land. In most manors, the custom is to divide the arable *land, land used for crops, into three large fields and then give strips of land from these fields to the peasants.*

Close to home

The villagers need little help from the outside world. They have a windmill to grind their grain, blacksmiths to shoe their horses and make tools, and a bakery.

The village church

Everyone must give part of his crop to the church. The people like the village priest, who allows them to dance in the churchyard, against the wishes of the bishop, who is miles away.

The peasants' rights
The peasants are allowed to take hay from their meadow, graze their animals on common land, and gather firewood in the forest, where their pigs can eat acorns.

The fun of the fair
The village fair provides great excitement twice a year. Traders buy the excellent wool produced at the manor and sell things that are not usually available in the village.

Song and dance
Some wandering players have arrived to entertain. A *jester*, or clown, dances with his dog, while another plays music to his dancing bear. A puppet theater attracts a small crowd.

The manor house
The lord of the manor's house is the largest of all the houses in the area, and usually built of stone. The steep roof has slates, and the windows are fitted with small panes of glass.

BROTHER WILLIAM'S MONASTERY

Following the dusty track leading over the river and out of the village, you find yourself looking down at the buildings of the monastery.

During the Middle Ages, many people devoted their lives to God by becoming monks and nuns. These people made serious vows in which they promised to serve God and give up the comforts of ordinary life. Prayer took up a major part of their day, but they also had to provide food for the monastery or nunnery by farming and to look after the poor and sick from local villages.

In a monastery, the abbot was the head of the monks, or brothers. He led the services in the abbey and organized the many people working for the monastery, not all of whom were monks.

A different world

On these pages, you can see that life in a medieval monastery is far from quiet. The lord of the manor's younger brother, William, is a monk, and as the new father prior, he assists the abbot.

Early to bed, early to rise
The monks sleep on hard wooden beds in a *dormitory*, a large room with many beds. To make time for the many services during the day, the brothers go to bed at sunset and rise early in the morning.

Fertile monastery gardens
The monks breed animals for meat and grow crops in some of the fields. There is an orchard and a walled vegetable garden. The monks grow many herbs for the kitchen and as medicines.

Silent prayer and noisy meetings
The *cloister* is a quiet square surrounded by *colonnades*, covered walks supported by pillars, where the monks can go during times of private prayer. Monks copy books by hand in the library and discuss the day-to-day business in the *chapter house.*

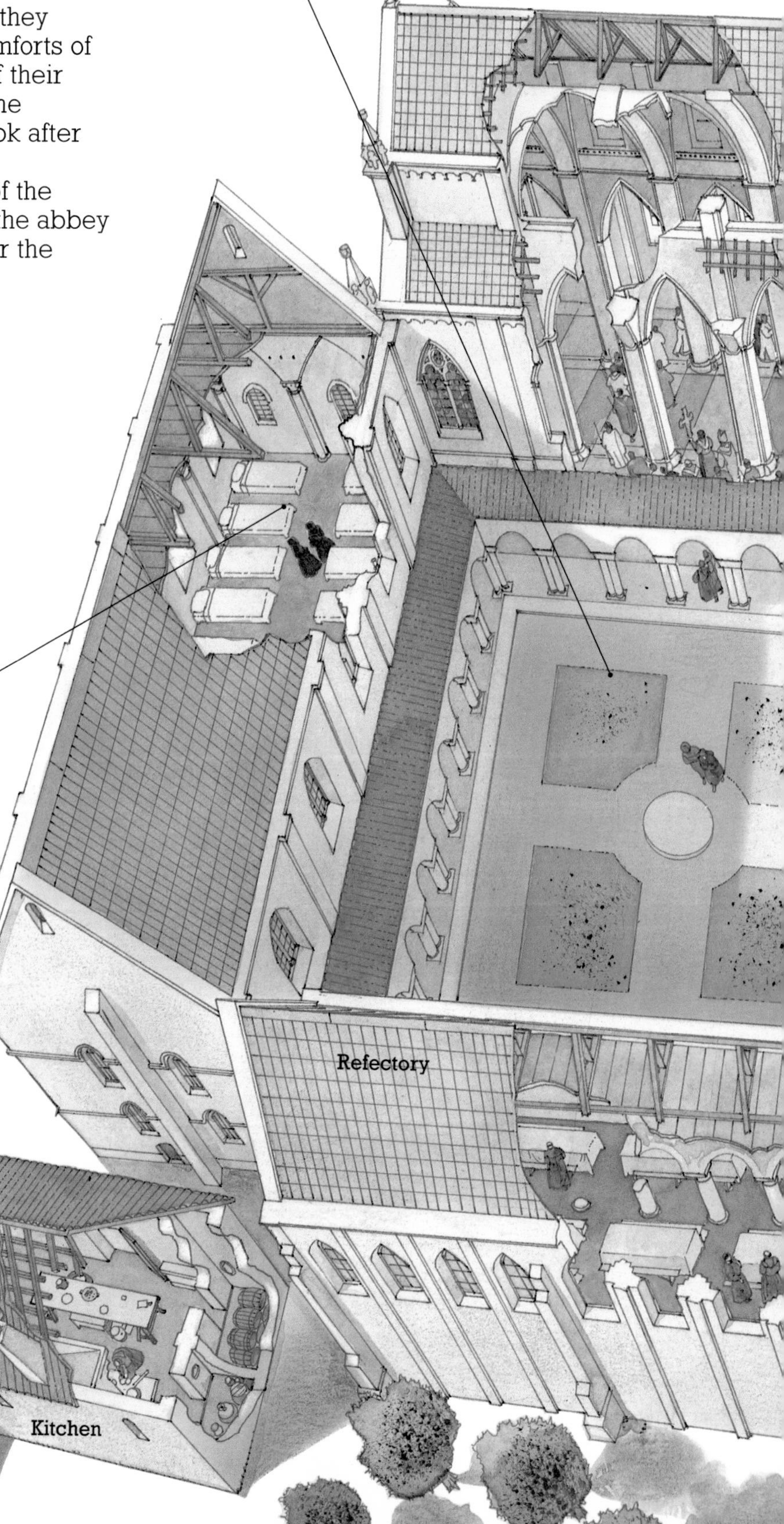

The abbey
There are three services during the day and then *vespers* at sunset and *compline* at bedtime. People travel for miles to see the abbey's most precious *relic*, or holy remains, a piece of Christ's cross.

The wealth of the church
The monastery is wealthy. Brother William rents out any fields not being used. Some noblemen, merchants, and rich traders also give money to the monastery.

Eating habits
The monks eat together in the *refectory* while one of them reads aloud from a religious book. Brother Dennis, as the *almoner*, provides food and clothing for the poor.

Comforting strangers
The abbot has his own house, where important visitors stay. It is also the duty of the monks to offer hospitality to travelers, so Brother Paul, as the *hospitaler*, arranges this.

Caring for the sick
The *infirmary* is where the monks look after their sick or aged brother monks. It is Brother Peter's job as the *infirmarer* to oversee nursing for the sick men who visit the monastery.

The school
There is a school to teach the *novices*, young boys training to become monks. Other boys are sent by their parents for an education because there are no other schools.

THE ITALIAN RENAISSANCE

You have headed southeast across the English Channel, through France and into northern Italy. It is AD 1450, and you are in the town of San Vitale during a time called the Renaissance.

The Renaissance, which means "rebirth," started in Italy but spread to most of Europe. It lasted from about AD 1450 until 1650. During this period, a new way of thinking blossomed. People living in medieval Europe had not questioned the world around them but during the renaissance they wanted to understand everything: the universe, nature, and how their bodies worked. Fascinated by ancient Greece and Rome, they studied the art, architecture, and philosophy of those times.

Northern Italian cities were wealthy from trade. There were rich *patrons*, men who supported great Renaissance artists, such as Leonardo da Vinci and Michelangelo, and encouraged them to create marvelous works of art.

A successful man in San Vitale
Here you can see into the world of the wealthy Renaissance banker Francesco Gattadoro and his family. He is an important man in the town, and the tradesmen treat him with great respect.

Cloth merchant

Working together
The *guilds*, groups of skilled workers who joined together in the Middle Ages to protect their crafts, still exist in San Vitale. Each trade has its own area in the town.

A touch of spice
Producing wool and making cloth and leather goods are San Vitale's important trades. Some merchants do business with Eastern traders and sell rare spices.

Furs and finery
The wealthy citizens wear embroidered clothes decorated with furs and fine jewelry, accompanied by elaborate headdresses. The poorer people dress in plain woolen cloth.

A true picture
Francesco drops in to see his new portrait. The artist has painted his patron with great realism, and Fancesco likes the way he appears in it, holding a small Roman statue.

The printed word
This craftsman has come from Germany with a new invention – a printing press. He can print a book in a few days. Before, it took months to copy a book by hand.

Local bargains
The shops open out on to the streets through archways, similar to those in ancient Rome. San Vitale's cloth shop is well stocked because northern Italy is famous for its wool.

Value for money
The Christian Church disapproves of charging fees for loans. Nonetheless, Francesco's bank, which lends money, is now an essential part of the town and has many customers.

Plasterers and painters
Skilled men are working on a new brick building. They have used thin layers of marble to decorate the outside of the top story, and they are plastering a lower wall for a fresco.

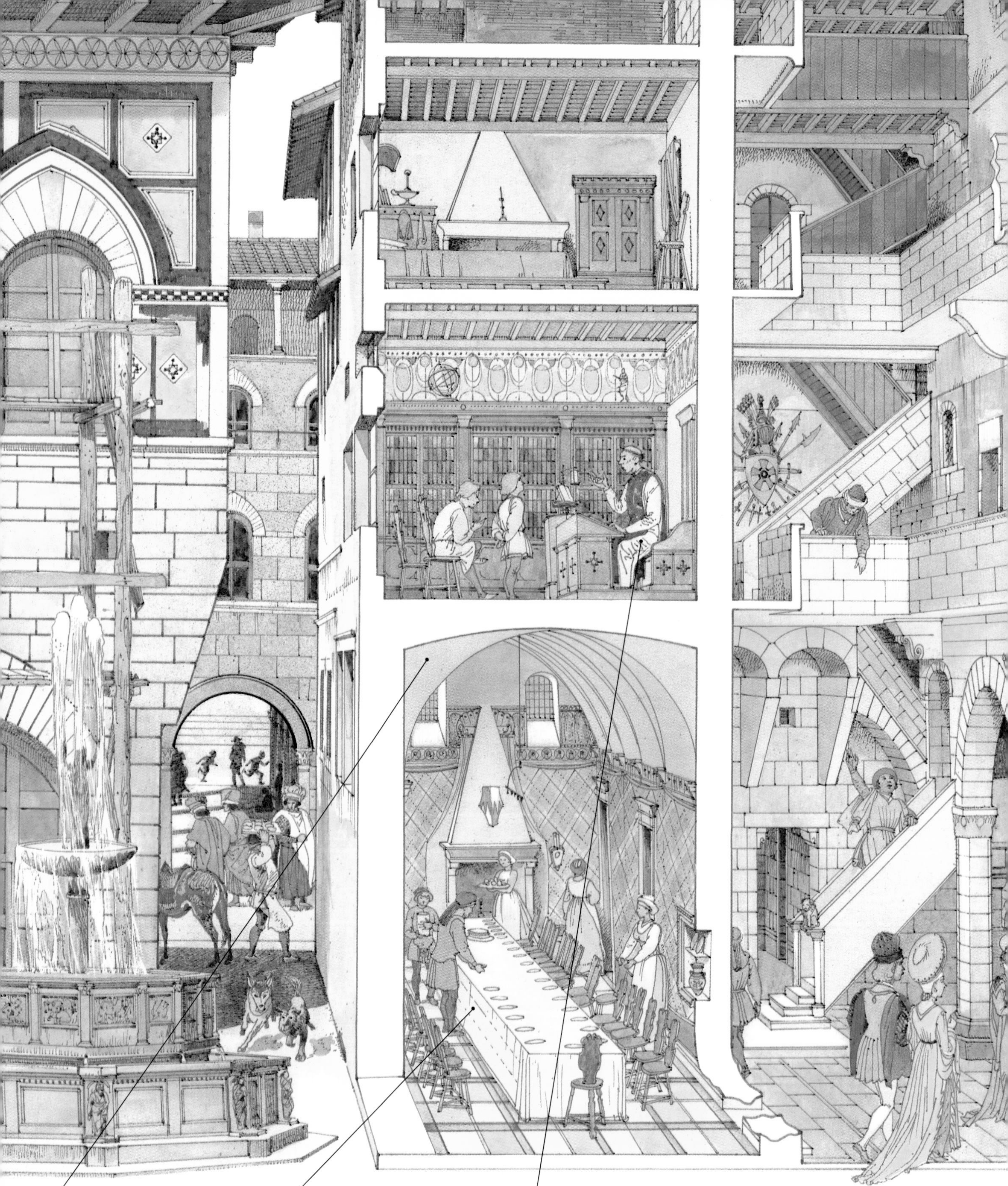

Echoes of Rome
Francesco's house shows his love of ancient Roman architecture. There are arches and pillars, and the banquet room has a *barrel-vaulted* ceiling, with arches in a tunnel shape.

A table for 40
Servants set the table with glass jugs and goblets made locally, silverware, and painted dishes. Forks are a new addition; before, people used knives, spoons, and their fingers.

A schoolroom
Francesco makes sure that his son Giovanni is highly educated. He employs a priest to teach science, mathematics, history, Greek and Latin. Katrina is also an excellent scholar.

Renaissance manners
Besides his normal studies, Giovanni writes poems, sings, plays the lute, hunts, and is taught chivalry. Such skills and manners are admired and respected in these times.

A question of power

Here you can see inside Francesco's grand house, called a palazzo, *which looks out on to a fountain in one of the main squares in San Vitale. The house is full of people because Francesco is giving a lavish banquet to celebrate the engagement of his daughter Katrina. He has chosen for her a rich husband who is connected to the great Medici family, which rules the nearby city of Florence.*

Like most rich Renaissance men, Francesco knows that his position of power depends on the success of his business and on having powerful friends. a closer link to the plans and actions of the powerful Medici family will help.

Living in style
Francesco's house is luxurious; the rooms are decorated with frescoes and wall hangings. Over the fireplace are stone mantles. Upstairs, the ceilings are wooden.

Sitting comfortably
Francesco has an office where he can talk business in private. Its wooden furniture is made with decorative panels.

Getting ready
Up in the study, a poet is preparing a poem to entertain the guests, who have assembled in the garden.

In the shade
Behind the palazzo is a large garden, carefully designed to display Francesco's marble statues. A covered walkway and trees provide welcome shade.

CLUES TO THE PAST

About 150 years ago, archaeology was treated like a treasure hunt and some of the people looking for treasure were little better than robbers. Other people collected less valuable items, such as flint spearheads, simply because they found them interesting. But there were also people who realized that if they carefully excavated an area of land where people settled centuries ago, they could discover a lot about the lives of those settlers.

Today, archaeologists are more like detectives, using the latest scientific equipment to help unravel clues to the past. When excavating, or "on a dig," they carefully remove the soil with brushes and special tools to avoid damaging remains or overlooking clues. They record every detail about a site and study everything they find, however broken or small, so they gradually build up a picture of how people lived. Every clue they find is vital, whether it is a coin, a ship, or a broken pot.

Buried treasure

Remains from other times can be preserved for hundreds or thousands of years, depending on luck or on the conditions in which they are buried. Here you can see what can be discovered.

Stepping-stones to history
Some ancient buildings are still standing, but most have been reduced to ruins or buried underground. An archaeologist needs skill and training to know how to reconstruct a ruined building and to find out how and why it was built.

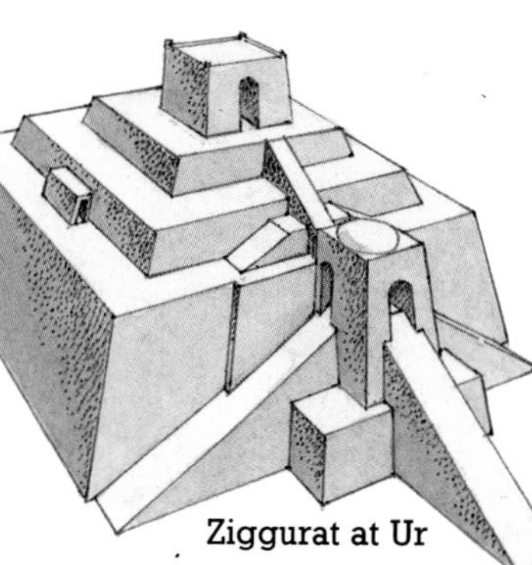

Ziggurat at Ur

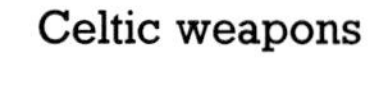

Celtic weapons

Secrets from the dead
Unless they are intentionally mummified, human bodies decay when they are buried in the ground. But some special conditions – hot sand, a bog, or ice – will preserve them, making it possible to tell what the people looked like, what they wore, and why they died.

Peat-bog man

War and peace
Finding many weapons on a site or in tombs usually means that the people were either warlike by nature or under constant threat of attack. Tools show how the people worked the land and how skilled the artisans were.

Games for eternity
Toys often give clues about the world in which children once lived. Archaeologists in Egypt have also found models showing such activites as preparing food, that were buried with the dead person to help him or her in the afterlife.

Egyptian wall painting

Egyptian toy boat

A colorful past
The tomb paintings found in Egypt and sometimes elsewhere give us a picture of the daily lives and religious beliefs of the people buried there.

Cretan statuette

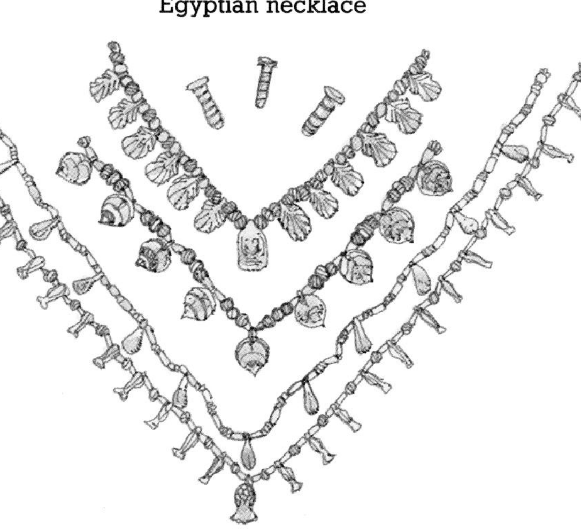
Egyptian necklace

Greek pot

A small fortune
Jewelry and objects made of precious stones and metals tell us about the wealth of their owners and the skill of their makers. We try to find out where they were made and if the gems were imported. If so, how were they paid for, or were they stolen?

Figure it out
Statues of kings and noblemen give us clues about their appearance, clothes, artistic tastes, and even their characters. Statues tell us how people imagined their gods, and shrines reveal how they worshiped.

Historical pots
Pottery provides useful clues. It had little value, so tomb robbers ignored it. Modern equipment can date it accurately, and since pots were not handed down from one generation to the next, objects found with them can also be dated.

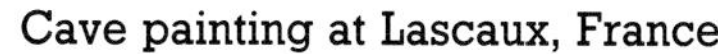
Cave painting at Lascaux, France

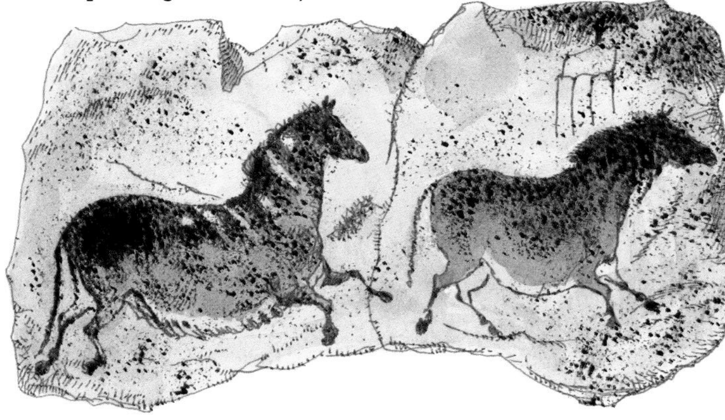

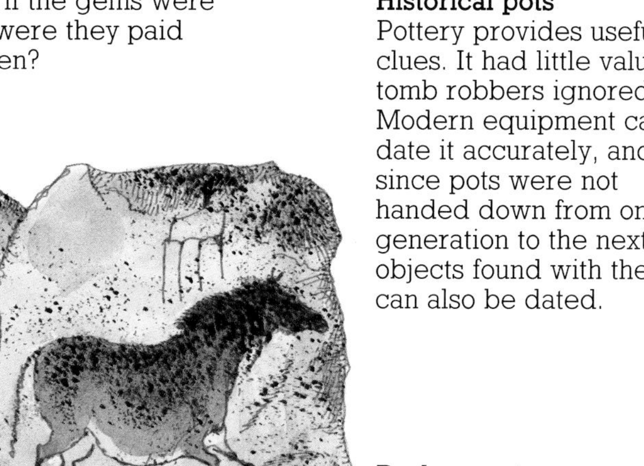

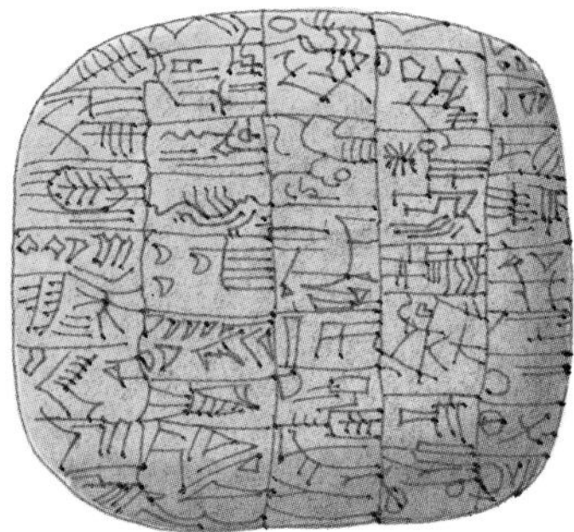
Writing on a tablet from Ur

Read between the lines
The written word is the most valuable source of information, but some writing is very hard to decipher. When writing can be read, archaeologists must remember that rulers often "bent" the truth.

Magic paintings
Cave paintings are superb decorations, but people now think they were done for another purpose. Did the painters believe they could magically increase the numbers of animals, or did the paintings bring the hunters good luck?

Dark secrets
Most people from the past believed in a life after death and hoped to take their possessions with them by having them placed in their tombs. As a result, tombs give archaeologists a lot of information, as long as robbers have not been there first.

Roman coins

Heads or tails?
Coins are useful because the rulers pictured on them help us give a date to the site in which they are found. Coins found far away from where they were made are a puzzle. Were they paid to foreign soldiers, used in trade, or were they raiders' loot?

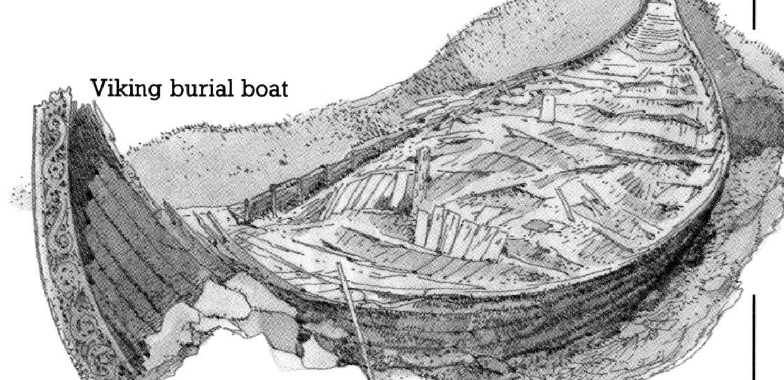
Viking burial boat

INDEX